Boyd's Guide to

Northeast Georgia's

Rabun County

◆

*Dozens of exciting things to see and do
in Georgia's most beautiful county.*

Brian A. Boyd

Fern Creek Press • Clayton, Georgia

Boyd's Guide to Northeast Georgia's Rabun County

Brian A. Boyd

ISBN #1-893651-14-2
Published and distributed by:
Fern Creek Press
PO Box 1322
Clayton, GA 30525
(706) 782-5379

Printed in the United States of America.

The author and publisher of this guidebook assume no responsibility for any loss of property, accident, injury or death sustained while visiting any of the locations described herein. Use all safety precautions and common sense when in the wild.

On the cover: One of the spectacular overlooks at Rabun County's Tallulah Gorge State Park.

Rabun County – *the best of North Georgia*

Often times the greatest discoveries of life are made while busy pursuing other interests. When a discovery comes by chance or accident, it makes the find all the more satisfying. Such was the case with my "discovery" of magnificent Rabun County over a quarter-century ago.

As a teenager, Rabun County, known then only as that place where *"Deliverance"* was filmed, was somewhat of a mystery. Like many other ignorant folks, the film's portrayal of inbred mountain men roaming the backwoods in search of a little quality time was enough to send a shiver down my spine. Sure, I'd driven through as a child, and spent quite a few nights with the folks dining at the Dillard House, but what lay beyond the sight of our automobile's window was of no great interest to me.

That all changed in the late 1970s during a hiking trip with a group of college buddies. My first real taste of Rabun's bounties came during several days spent on the magnificent Bartram & Chattooga River Trail, and it was love at first sight.

The sights, sounds and even smells of these mountains went straight to my head. If there was any doubt that I had fallen in love with this county, it was put to rest after my first intoxicating experiences (figuratively, of course) on the incomparable Chattooga Wild and Scenic River. I was sure that one day I would find a way here and make Rabun County my home, a dream finally realized in 1991.

This outdoor paradise is a land of rugged, time-worn peaks, rolling ridges and serene, picturesque valleys. It is a land of mighty and *once-*mighty rivers, a land of sparkling streams and of majestic, dancing waterfalls. Rabun County is an enchanting land created for exploration and appreciated by anyone who loves God's creation.

This magnificent county boasts many impressive natural features. Consider a few of Rabun's natural wonders - like Rabun Bald, Georgia's second

3

highest mountain (4,696'); or Sky Valley, the highest valley in the state and one of the loftiest incorporated towns in the eastern U.S. Then there's Tallulah Gorge, perhaps the most rugged gorge in the East with a depth of nearly 1,000 feet. One of our biggest draws is the incomparable Chattooga River, which forms Rabun's eastern boundary with South Carolina. And this is just the beginning.

Add to this the fact that over 60% of Rabun's 236,000+ acres is owned by the U.S. Forest Service and about 8% is controlled by Georgia Power Company and you come to one inescapable conclusion - there's plenty of room to roam in Rabun County!

If wilderness isn't your thing, consider that Rabun is Georgia's only county to feature three, count 'em, three, state parks - Tallulah Gorge State Park, Black Rock Mountain State Park, and Moccasin Creek State Park. These three jewels offer three delightfully different outdoor experiences.

Rabun also boasts an incomparable string of sparkling mountain lakes along the ancient Tallulah River.

Generations of fishing and boating enthusiasts have prized these lakes since just after the turn of the 20th century. The names are familiar - Burton, Seed (or Nacoochee), Rabun, Tallulah, and Tugalo are all popular and quite well-known around the Southeast. Boating, skiing, swimming and fishing are all top-notch on these wonderful mountain treasures.

Not to be left out, fishing and hunting are quite popular here as well. Rabun County features miles of stocked trout streams. The crowds flock primarily to just a few - the upper Tallulah, and the northern portions of the Chattooga and the West Fork in particular, but many more lesser well known streams are waiting for anglers of all skill levels. Hunters will enjoy thousands of acres of managed game lands such as the Warwoman Wildlife Management Area where a variety of game awaits.

Regardless of your passion, if it involves the great outdoors, it can most likely be enjoyed to perfection in Rabun County. So how about it? On your next trip up, get out of the car and live a little. You'll be glad you visited our county. I know I was.

Before you go

A word to the wise concerning personal safety

While ever-increasing numbers of visitors flock to the northeast Georgia mountains each year, the area nonetheless remains somewhat wild and potentially dangerous. Numerous deaths and scores of injuries occur annually because of accidents, poor preparation, and often downright stupid behavior.

Waterfall safety: By far the most dangerous attractions in the northeast Georgia mountains are waterfalls. Truly, these wonders of nature are spectacular to behold. However, each year people are seriously injured or killed attempting to climb **onto** the falls. Please be content to view our waterfalls from the safety of observation decks or from a safe area at the base of the falls.

Also, never attempt to cross a river or stream on foot, particularly at high water. The power of moving water is quite deceptive, and there have been numerous instances of deaths due to foot entrapment on the Chattooga River.

General safety: Please obey all posted rules and regulations when in the Chattahoochee National Forest, state parks, recreation areas or wilderness areas.

If possible, do not hike alone, and always let someone else know where you are going and when you expect to return. If possible, carry a first-aid kit and know how to use it.

Be aware of changing weather conditions, especially the possibility of lightning during the summer thunderstorm season.

Always lock your automobile and store any valuables in the trunk where they cannot be seen. Trailhead parking areas in particular are frequent sites of break-ins. Take every precaution to safeguard your valuables.

About this guide...

It is quite likely that some of the descriptions included in this guidebook will become obsolete or possibly even erroneous at some point. Construction, improvements, natural disasters and even closure sometimes occur in natural areas open to visitors. If you encounter anything which you believe to be in error, please contact Fern Creek Press. We'd like to correct any misinformation for the safety and enjoyment of future visitors.

Much of the information in this guide is quite subjective. For instance, the trail ratings may be open to various interpretations. Generally speaking, **easy** means that practically anyone can hike a particular trail, including grandma (that is, as long as grandma can get around ok). **Moderate** means that the participant should expect at least some physical exertion (couch potatoes will do some sweating, but should be alright). **Strenuous** means that you better be in pretty good physical condition or you will regret it. Also keep in mind that elevation changes are at least as

important (in difficulty ratings) as mileage figures. A 1,000' change in elevation may be beyond the average beginner's ability. A good example of this is the hike down into Tallulah Gorge. You may not be able to discern those who fit the "out-of-shape" category by watching hikers descend into the gorge, but they become very obvious during the climb out. (They are usually draped across boulders clutching their hearts and gasping for breath.) Know your fitness level before attempting any unfamiliar hike, and **never hike alone!**

Though trail maps are included in this publication, any hike into the wilderness should include Forest Service maps or U.S. Geological Survey maps. And even with the best and most updated information there is absolutely no substitute for good common sense. Get as many of the details as you can, and **be prepared for anything when in the outdoors**. Have a great time, but be safe!

Inside the guide...

- **Introduction** 3
- **Section One – Rabun's State Parks** 9
  - Tallulah Gorge State Park 10
  - Black Rock Mountain State Park 18
  - Moccasin Creek State Park 25
- **Section Two – The Chattooga River** 29
  - Background 30
  - Burrells Ford 31
  - Russell Bridge 35
  - Sandy Ford 39
  - U.S. 76 Bridge 44
  - Chattooga River Trail 48
  - Lower Chattooga 52
  - Chattooga Boating Information 58
- **Section Three – National Forest Destinations** 61
  - Fall Branch Trail 62
  - Joe Branch Trail 64
  - Warwoman Dell Recreation Area 66
  - Falls on Martin Creek 68
  - Stonewall Biking Trails 70
  - Coleman River Trail 72
  - Tate City and the upper Tallulah 74
  - Denton Branch Falls 76
  - Beech Creek Gorge 77
  - Appalachian Trail 80
  - Popcorn Overlook 83
  - Wildcat Creek 84
  - Willis Knob Horse Trail and Camp 85
  - Holcomb Creek Trail 86
  - Rabun Bald 88
  - Three Forks 91
  - Bartram Trail 94
- **Section Four – Other Great Destinations** 99
  - The Great Lakes 100
  - Paddling the Tallulah River 105
  - Trout Streams of Rabun 108
  - Campgrounds 111
  - Foxfire Museum 114
  - Tallulah Falls Railroad Museum 115
  - Hambidge Center 116
  - Barker's Creek Mill 117
  - Estatoah Falls and Mud Creek Falls 118
  - Ellicott Rock Wilderness 119
  - Sightseeing by Automobile 120
- **Section Five – Additional Information** 123
  - Emergency Numbers 123
  - Commercial Numbers of Interest 124
  - Seasonal Special Events 126

Table of Contents

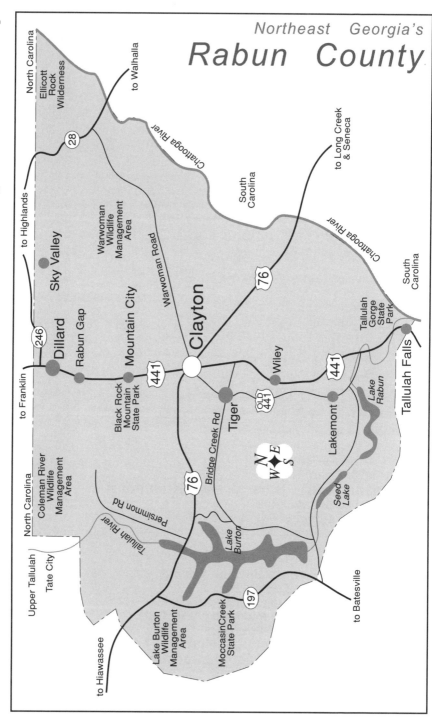

Northeast Georgia's

Rabun County

Section One

Rabun County's State Parks

- Tallulah Gorge State Park   10
- Black Rock Mountain State Park   18
- Moccasin Creek State Park   25

The wall of water at Sliding Rock –
Tallulah Gorge State Park

Tallulah Gorge State Park
Dramatic beauty and rich history make Tallulah a favorite

The north rim overlook above Hawthorne's Pool and Ladore Falls.

**Tallulah Gorge State Park
P.O. Box 248
Tallulah Falls, GA 30573
(706) 754-7970
www.gastateparks.org**

- Magnificent scenery
- Five major waterfalls
- Hiking and biking
- Day use area
- Arts center
- Jane Hurt Yarn Interpretive Center
- Entrance fee required

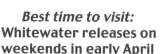

***Best time to visit:*
Whitewater releases on weekends in early April and early November!**

E stablished in 1992, Tallulah Gorge State Park is one of Georgia's newest state parks, and is without doubt one of our state's most outstanding. Jointly developed by the Georgia Department of Natural Resources and the Georgia Power Company, Tallulah Gorge State Park offers arguably the most dramatic landscapes in Georgia, principally Tallulah Gorge and its unmatched collection of rugged cliffs and waterfalls.

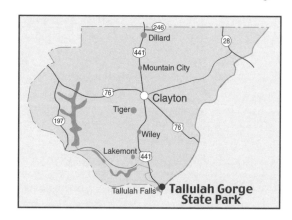

This spectacular natural chasm - nearly 1,000 feet deep and more than two miles long - was carved over time by the powerful waters of the once-mighty Tallulah River.

Though the park is relatively new, Tallulah Gorge has attracted those seeking beauty and adventure for nearly 200 years. Today's Tallulah Gorge offers one of the most unique educational and recreational opportunities to be found anywhere in the Southeastern United States.

96-foot Hurricane Falls

Accommodations: Fifty tent and recreational vehicle sites are available. Call (706) 754-7979 for reservations. All sites are available on a first-come, first-served basis.

The dramatic suspension bridge at the brink of Hurricane Falls.

Jane Hurt Yarn Interpretive Center: This magnificent 16,000 sq. ft. facility contains cultural, historical and natural exhibits pertaining to Tallulah Gorge and Tallulah Falls. The center features a gift shop, classroom facilities and a theater which regularly airs a professionally produced video on the gorge. Gorge access permits and restricted trails permits must be acquired here.

11

The dramatic landscape of the inner gorge.

Georgia Heritage Center for the Arts: This gallery contains an excellent collection of art from across the region. Inquire for hours of operation.

Terrora Day-Use Area: Before Tallulah Gorge became a state park, this area was operated by Georgia Power Company as Terrora Park. Situated along the picturesque shores of 63-acre Tallulah Lake, Terrora features a beach, picnic area with playground, and tennis courts. The day use area is located along the highway just north of the bridge.

Hiking and Biking Trails: The park features a variety of hiking and biking trails ranging from easy to very difficult. Detailed information and trail maps may be obtained at the interpretive center information desk. **Be aware that several of the trails require permits**.

Rim Trails: The official starting point for this walk is the Yarn Interpretive Center. Both the **North** and **South Rim Trails** are approximately 0.75 mile one way, making a complete hike on each trail about 1.5 miles. Each offers a variety of excellent overlooks and impressive vistas. The **North Rim Trail** features excellent views of Oceana and Ladore Falls, and runs roughly from

Beautiful Ladore Falls as seen from the north rim trail

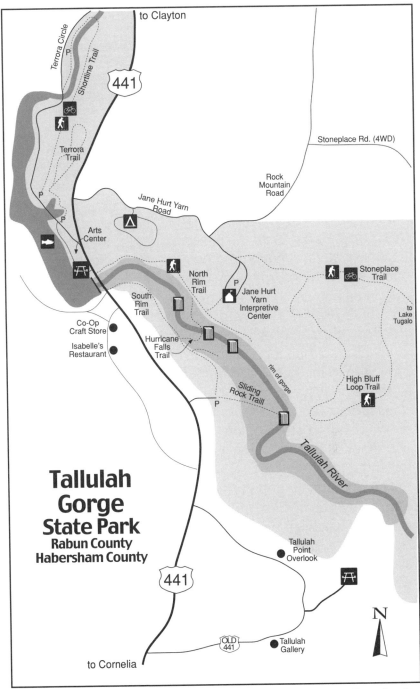

to Clayton

Terrora Circle

Shortline Trail

441

Terrora Trail

Stoneplace Rd. (4WD)

Rock Mountain Road

Jane Hurt Yarn Road

Arts Center

North Rim Trail

Jane Hurt Yarn Interpretive Center

Stoneplace Trail

to Lake Tugalo

South Rim Trail

Co-Op Craft Store

Isabelle's Restaurant

Hurricane Falls Trail

rim of gorge

High Bluff Loop Trail

Sliding Rock Traill

Tallulah River

Tallulah Gorge State Park
Rabun County
Habersham County

441

Tallulah Point Overlook

OLD 441

Tallulah Gallery

N

to Cornelia

Detailed park maps are available at the Yarn Interpretive Center

the Yarn Interpretive Center to the Highway 441 bridge at Tallulah dam.

The **South Rim Trail** begins beyond the bridge, winding past a covered overlook along a pathway originally built for one of the grand hotels of the 1800s. Excellent views of Hawthorne's Pool and cliffs, Tempesta Falls and Hurricane Falls can be enjoyed along this walk.

For those in good shape, a shortcut connects the two trails. The **Hurricane Falls Trail** requires a descent of several hundred steps to access a dramatic suspension bridge strung just above the brink of mighty Hurricane Falls. During water releases, the hike is particularly worthwhile, as thundering curtains of spray shroud the gorge floor.

Descending the stairs along the Hurricane Falls Trail

Those seeking an even greater workout can continue from the suspension bridge to the base of Hurricane Falls, another several hundred steps below, for a magnificent view from the gorge floor. Be advised, the ascent from this point is extremely challenging!

The immensely popular **Shortline Trail** is located in the Terrora day-use section of the park. This 1.5 mile (one way) paved trail follows the railbed of the abandoned Tallulah Falls Railroad through a series of cuts and fills along the beautiful Tallulah River upstream of the dam and gorge. This easy pathway is a favorite among joggers, walkers, and bikers, and is highlighted by a long suspension bridge arched over the splashing river. Small parking areas are located at either end, both along Terrora Circle.

Also accessed from the southern end of the Shortline Trail are the moderately easy 1 mile **Terrora Loop Trail** and the 0.5 mile **Lake Trail**, which has an alternate trailhead at the old jail adjacent to the abandoned railway bridge. Both of these trails, while not dramatic, feature enjoyable forest walks with splashing creeks and gently rolling terrain.

Trails Requiring Permits

The scenic **High Bluff Trail** loops away from the Interpretive Center for several miles through a south-facing forest above the north rim along a series of old road beds.

The challenging **Stoneplace Trail** (5 miles one way) descends along a series of old logging roads to a primitive camping area on the western shoreline of beautiful Lake Tugalo. This pathway is great for hikers and bikers alike, but is rated as challenging due to a descent of approximately 800 vertical feet.

The wildly popular but challenging **Wallenda Trail** (aka Sliding Rock Trail) leads to Sliding Rock. Though only about 0.25 mile long, it descends over rugged bare rock, dropping about 600 vertical feet. **Sliding Rock**, also known as Bridal Veil Falls, features a thrilling slide into a broad pool nestled against imposing granite cliffs. This is a dangerous area and many injuries attest to the fact that this is true wilderness and must be respected.

Those with a gorge floor permit may explore upstream along the rugged riverbed up to Hurricane Falls. Here hikers may access the staircase leading up to the gorge rim. Use extreme caution along this section of the gorge floor, as slippery rocks and rugged terrain create a myriad of dangerous obstacles. Of particular note is a massive rock wall which forms Oceana Falls, located a few hundred yards downstream of Hurricane Falls.

The wild ride at Sliding Rock

Tallulah Falls... A Rich History

Since the early 1900s visitors to the southern Blue Ridge have stopped at the overlooks along Old U.S. Highway 23/441 and gazed into the foreboding abyss that is Tallulah Gorge. Even though the bulk of travelers head farther north to the more popular tourist destinations, a quick stop to take in the view of Tallulah Gorge is almost a requirement, for here is where the Blue Ridge seems to first rise up. Most encounters with Tallulah Gorge end here, but

Hikers in Tallulah Gorge in the early 1900s.

this was not always so; and with the establishment of Tallulah Gorge State Park, the mighty gorge is once again a prime destination rather than a mere curiosity.

Tallulah Gorge began attracting sightseers shortly after the native Cherokees were driven out in the early 1800s. The gorge was a rugged 12 mile hike from the nearest town of Clarkesville, but by the mid-1800s a growing number of visitors made the trek to witness Tallulah's wonders. A number of primitive "inns" began to spring up to accommodate the growing interest in the gorge.

The first real commercialization of Tallulah Gorge began around 1870 with the opening of the Shirley Hotel, built about a mile from the gorge. By the early 1880s Tallulah Falls had become a boomtown, spurred by an onslought of visitors wishing to view this natural wonder. Eventually around 17 hotels and boarding houses, including many beautiful Victorians, called Tallulah Falls home. Much of this was spurred by the arrival of the Tallulah Falls Railroad in 1882. Tallulah Falls, the "Niagara of the South" had become one of the prime tourist resorts of the Blue Ridge.

The combination of the rugged gorge and its magnificent collection of superb waterfalls provided all the ingredients for continuing development. Unfortunately for the town, the same dramatic landscape also attracted those interested in harnessing the power of the Tallulah River for hydroelectric power.

A tremendous environmental fight took place in the early 1900s to save the Gorge from developers proposing a series of dams. The result of this fight, Tallulah Falls dam, was completed in 1913. Two massive tunnels diverted most of the Tallulah River's powerful flow to a hydroelectric plant near the lower end of the gorge. The waterfalls of the inner gorge all but disappeared and with them most of the tourism.

Karl Wallenda crossing Tallulah Gorge in 1970

The railroad was extended to Franklin, North Carolina, in the early 1900s, and a series of fires in the 1920s and 1930s left the town of Tallulah Falls and the beautiful hotels all but destroyed. The gorge, which was once alive with the power of the mighty Tallulah, became a place of silent beauty.

Little of great interest took place in Tallulah Falls until 1970, when the daring aerialist Karl Wallenda took his famous walk over Tallulah Gorge. Today Tallulah Gorge has once again become a popular destination. Due to a minimum flow which regularly runs through the gorge and scheduled whitewater releases several times each year, the great falls live once again. With with the establishment of the park in 1992, Tallulah Gorge has once again regained its rightful prominence.

An in-depth history of Tallulah Falls and Tallulah Gorge can be found in *"Secrets of Tallulah,"* available from Fern Creek Press. Call (706) 782-5379 for details.

Black Rock Mountain State Park

Georgia's highest state park offers incrdible vistas

Spectacular mid-winter view from Cowee Overlook

Black Rock Mountain State Park
P.O. Drawer A
Mountain City, GA 30562
(706) 746-21 41
www.gastateparks.org

- **Magnificent scenery**
- **Six peaks above 3,000' elevation**
- **Great hiking trails**
- **Picnic tables & pavilions**
- **Camping & cottages**
- **Fishing lake**
- **Entrance fee required**

Best time to visit:
Fall leaf looking is spectacular...summers offer a cool escape

Black Rock Mountain State Park derives its name from the smooth, sheer cliffs of dark granite located just below the park's mountaintop visitor center. In a region that features a number of outstanding parks, Black Rock Mountain State Park has the distinction of being the highest state park in Georgia. Encompassing over 1,718 acres and featuring six peaks that reach above the lofty 3,000' level, Black Rock Mountain State Park is situated squarely astride the eastern continental divide and offers a wealth of scenery that is nothing short of spectacular.

The focal point of the park is its lofty visitor center, perched atop a sheer cliff that gazes down nearly 2,000 vertical feet onto the picturesque town of Clayton and affords views well into the foothills region of South Carolina. If you're looking for beauty without the crowds, Black Rock may be just your ticket.

Accommodations:

Black Rock Mountain State Park offers a surprisingly large number of accommodations for overnight visitors, including 10 rental cottages, a 48-site campground for tents and recreational vehicles, a walk-in campsite, pioneer camping and several backcountry sites.

Beautiful 17–acre Black Rock Lake is a favorite destination for anglers

Black Rock Lake: It might seem a bit odd that a park known for its lofty peaks would also feature a sizeable lake, but that's exactly what you'll find here. Seventeen-acre Black Rock Lake, constructed in 1974, is located on the northwestern corner of the park. Situated some 1,400 vertical feet below the summit of Black Rock Mountain, the lake (elevation 2,241') offers surprisingly good fishing for bass, bream, catfish and trout.

Picnicking: Several large covered pavilions and an ample scattering of picnic tables are found in the wooded area around the mountaintop visitor center. Adjacent to one of the pavilions is a playground that kids of all ages are sure to enjoy. Pavilions may be reserved in advance for large groups. Call for details.

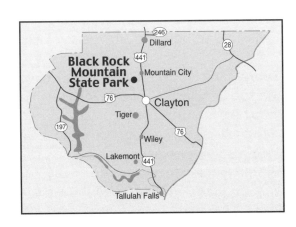

Hiking Trails: Black Rock Mountain State Park has one of the most scenic and challenging trail systems of any of Georgia's state parks. Over 10 miles of developed trails lace the park, with each offering a dramatically different hiking experience.

The magnificent vista from the Blue Ridge Overlook

Ada-hi Falls Trail: This 0.25 mile (one way) trail descends approximately 200 vertical feet to tiny Ada-hi Falls, a noisy cascade high in the Taylor Creek watershed. The walk takes one through a shady, north-facing hardwood cove featuring a variety of ferns and wildflowers. The trailhead is located just a short walk from the trading post and amphitheater. Visitors should be aware that Ada-hi Falls can all but disappear during prolonged periods of dry weather.

Another pathway connects the Ada-hi Falls trailhead with the parking area for the park's longer trails. The **Springhouse -Ada-hi Falls Trail** climbs up to the roadside springhouse just across Black Rock Mountain Parkway from the Edmonds-Tennessee Rock trailhead parking area. This trail allows hikers parked in the large upper parking area to access the Ada-hi Falls Trail without moving their vehicle.

Tennessee Rock Trail: The park's most popular hiking trail is the spectacular 2.2 mile Tennessee Rock Trail. This moderate loop hike features plenty of biological diversity and culminates with a jaw-dropping vista from atop 3,640' Black Rock Mountain.

This yellow-blazed trail begins in the parking area along Black Rock Mountain Parkway located just above the springhouse. Proceed into the woods, then bear right at the fork. The initial mile is along the steep, north-facing flanks

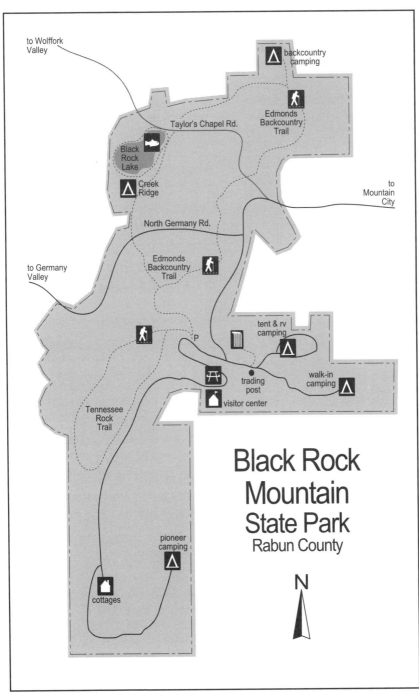

to Wolffork
Valley

backcountry
camping

Edmonds
Backcountry
Trail

Taylor's Chapel Rd.

Black
Rock
Lake

Creek
Ridge

to
Mountain
City

North Germany Rd.

Edmonds
Backcountry
Trail

to Germany
Valley

tent & rv
camping

P

walk-in
camping

trading
post

visitor center

Tennessee
Rock
Trail

Black Rock
Mountain
State Park
Rabun County

N

pioneer
camping

cottages

Detailed park maps are available at the park visitor center

21

A lone hiker atop magnificent Tennessee Rock.

below Black Rock Mountain's elongated ridgeline. This portion of the trail features a prolific variety of beautiful ferns, mosses and seasonal wildflowers, including several varieties of lovely trilliums.

The trail maintains a generally flat grade through the first 1.2 miles of the hike as it weaves through a mature hardwood forest punctuated by an Appalachian boulderfield. After passing through a fragrant grove of mature white pines, the path begins its 300-foot ascent to Black Rock Mountain's wind-swept summit ridgeline. The actual summit (3,640') isn't unusually dramatic, as it is heavily wooded and doesn't offer much of a view.

The highlight of this trail occurs a few hundred yards beyond at the Tennessee Rock Overlook (elevation 3,625'). Here a seemingly endless parade of time-worn peaks recede into the far western horizon. Beautiful Wolffork Valley is at your feet, and lofty peaks such as Georgia's Brasstown Bald and the Smokies' Clingman's Dome can be seen on extremely clear days. This is truly a spot to linger and enjoy - but protect your

Tennessee Rock Interpretive Guide

The park publishes a 32-page illustrated booklet "An Interpretive Guide to the Tennessee Rock Trail." This informative publication is available for a nominal cost at the park visitor center. The booklet provides useful information about the park's natural history, pioneer and Native American life, geology, geography, and climate. The publication's text corresponds to 25 numbered posts located along the trail.

children from the steep drop-off beyond the overlook railing.

The quarter-mile portion of the trail that runs along the ridgeline actually sits astride the Eastern Continental Divide. Rain falling to the north flows into the Little Tennessee River watershed and eventually into the Gulf of Mexico, while rain falling to the south of the trail flows into the Chattooga River basin, becomes part of the Savannah River, and eventually empties into the Atlantic Ocean. Your attention may be fixed upon the trail as it weaves through greyish boulders and gnarled rhododendrons, but superb views can be glimpsed off either side of the narrow ridge-line.

After making brief contact with Black Rock Mountain Parkway the trail descends rather quickly along the mountain's north slope to

The view from the visitor center includes Clayton and extends well into South Carolina on a clear day.

the original fork and the trailhead parking area just beyond.

James E. Edmonds Backcountry Trail: The park's most challenging trail was named in honor of one the first rangers here. This 7.2 mile loop trail features an elevation gain of over 1,000 vertical feet, so those who choose to attempt this trail need to be in excellent physical condition. While the park rates the average trail time as 4 hours, there are amusing stories of those who have taken quite a bit longer.

The Edmonds Trail shares the same trailhead as the Tennessee Rock Trail, so be sure to follow the signs carefully and make sure you are on the trail featuring orange blazes. Pick up one of the free trail maps provided by the park - it is the best way to be sure you have the most up-to-date information. The Edmonds Backcountry Trail doesn't feature a great deal of level hiking. Primarily the first 2.5 miles encompasses a general descent from around 3,300' at the trailhead to around 2,400' at Taylor Creek. The initial 0.7 mile descends to a fork. For purposes of this description, take the fork to the right.

From hard-core hikers the fun starts here, as the next half mile features an exhilarating 600-foot climb to rugged Scruggs Knob (elevation 3,048') and an impressive grove of twisted mountain laurel. At mile 3.5 a spur trail to the right climbs 0.7 mile to Lookoff Mountain (3,162'). Two backcountry campsites (permit required) are located in this area. Several overlooks are perched atop sheer granite cliffs and feature sublime views of Wolffork Valley and the ranges of the Blue Ridge beyond.

Once you have backtracked to the main Edmunds loop, it descends over the next mile down to a crossing of Taylor's Chapel Road around mile 4.5. This crossing occurs within site of beautiful 17-acre Black Rock Lake (2,241'). If you're not tired yet, try the .85 mile trail that circles the lake. Otherwise, you'd better take a breather.

After paralleling the southern shoreline of the lake, the trail passes the Creek Ridge Backcountry Campsite #4, then crosses and roughly follows noisy Greasy Creek upstream through lush rhododendron stands. A second footbridge over the creek signals the intersection with North Germany Road.

Beyond, the trail encounters a steep section that switchbacks as it climbs sharply back to the original trail fork. Retrace your steps along the original 0.7 mile segment of the trail, climbing several hundred vertical feet back to your waiting vehicle. Congratulations - you've conquered the Edmonds Backcountry Trail and experienced much of the park's very best scenery the old fashioned way - on foot!

Moccasin Creek State Park

Tiny Moccasin Creek is a gateway to beautiful Lake Burton

Moccasin Creek spills into beautiful Lake Burton

Moccasin Creek State Park
3655 GA Hwy 197
Clarkesville, GA 30523
(706) 947-3194
www.gastateparks.org

- **Fishing & boating**
- **Adjacent to fish hatchery**
- **Hiking trails**
- **Entrance fee required**

As you might expect, campsites can be very difficult to obtain on warm weather weekends.

Tiny Moccasin Creek State Park lies nestled in a broad cove along the northwestern shore of beautiful 2,800-acre Lake Burton. Though only 32 acres in size, Moccasin Creek offers a host of outstanding park amenities. The park's 1,866' elevation keeps it cool, even in the midst of a hot north Georgia summer, and with the Chattahoochee National Forest right next door, you know there will be plenty of recreational opportunities to enjoy.

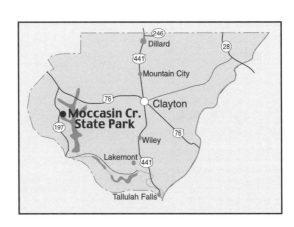

Accommodations: Campers absolutely love Moccasin Creek's 54 tent and trailer sites. The campground was planted with white pine trees during its early years, and visitors today reap the benefits via scores of mature trees which provide a blanket of cool shade. The campground is small, and each site is just a short walk from the lake and the other amenities.

Picnicking: Picnics are a favorite event at beautiful Moccasin Creek State Park. An open air pavilion and picnic area alongside the lake provide the perfect venue. Parents will also appreciate the large playground here.

Boating: Without a doubt, boating is one of the primary forms of recreation for those who frequent Moccasin Creek State Park. Lake Burton is known as one of the premier boating and fishing lakes in Georgia. The fish hatchery adjacent to the park features a public boat ramp and a private boat dock is available in the park for registered campers.

Didn't bring a boat? No problem. Lake Burton features several marinas for those who'd like to rent, whether it be a pontoon or ski boat. Inquire at park headquarters for the latest information.

Fishing: Cold, clear Moccasin Creek flows along the park's southern boundary, and is quite attractive to trout fishermen - but only a chosen few. Children 11 and younger may fish here, as well as seniors who possess an honorary license. The rest of us have to fish that portion of the

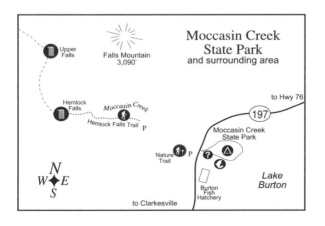

stream that lies west of the park. Be sure to abide by all posted regulations. There are certain portions of the stream that may be closed to the public. A word to the wise: better have your license in hand, as the authorities are fond of checking.

Burton Fish Hatchery: The Lake Burton Fish Hatchery is located just a stone's throw south of the park, right alongside Hwy. 197. This hatchery raises rainbow trout destined for streams and rivers across north Georgia. Children of all ages are fascinated by the thousands of hungry trout in various stages of growth and development. Hatchery hours are normally 8 am to 4:30 pm daily but may vary according to the season.

Hiking: A 1.1 mile nature loop is located just across Hwy. 197 from the park entrance, adjacent to the hatchery intake. This easy trail is perfect for children and adults alike. The more adventurous may wish to continue on the gravel road past the nature loop for 0.5 mile to the **Hemlock Falls Trail**. A relatively easy one mile (one way) trail utilizes an old logging roadbed up to this pretty 15-foot waterfall and its gorgeous emerald-green plunge pool.

The first 0.7 mile features a flat to moderate grade as the trail climbs above tumbling Moccasin Creek. A narrow foot-bridge carries hikers to the north side of the creek, then climbs along-side a series of impressive cascades and small waterfalls. About 0.3 mile beyond the foot-

Beautiful Hemlock Falls on Moccasin Creek

bridge pretty Hemlock Falls comes into view. Just prior to reaching the falls, the path veers and drops into a broad clearing leading up to the fall's huge plunge pool. Summer visitors may find the pool occupied with swimmers, but be forewarned - Moccasin Creek is COLD, even in the midst of the hottest summers. A convenient scattering of large rocks provides several good vantage points from which to view the falls, picnic, or just take in the atmosphere.

There are other cascades on Moccasin Creek well upstream of Hemlock Falls, but the trail becomes very hard to discern and hazardous stream crossings are required. Only experienced hikers with updated maps should proceed beyond Hemlock Falls.

Section 2 Two

The Chattooga Wild & Scenic River

- **Introduction to the Chattooga**   30
- **Burrells Ford**   31
- **Russell Bridge**   35
- **Sandy Ford**   39
- **U.S. 76 Bridge**   44
- **Chattooga River Trail**   48
- **Lower Chattooga**   52
- **Chattooga Boating Information**   58

Whitewater boating on rugged Section IV of the Chattooga River

The Chattooga River – background

Georgia's premier whitewater stream enjoys federal protection

The magnificent Chattooga River forms the eastern boundary of Georgia's Rabun County - nearly forty miles in all. The legendary Chattooga features some of the wildest whitewater in the eastern U.S., attracting thousands of boating enthusiasts into the Rabun County area.

The Chattooga River gained instant notoriety in the early 1970s due to the commercial success of the film, *Deliverance.* While Burt Reynolds, Jon Voigt and company may have created a whitewater monster, a new generation of hikers and fishermen have discovered the river as well. Today the Chattooga remains one of the Southeast's last free-flowing rivers, and offers those with a love of the outdoors an unmatched wilderness experience.

In 1968, the U.S. Congress passed the National Wild and Scenic Rivers Act, aimed at preserving our nation's most spectacular waterways. Under this act a river must be classified under the following categories:

Wild - unpolluted, undammed, with primitive surroundings - accessible only by foot.
Scenic - undammed, with undeveloped shoreline, accessible by road.
Recreational - easily accessible by road with some development and pre-existing dams allowed.

The Chattooga joined the National Wild and Scenic River System in 1974. Of the river's 57 mile length, 40 miles are classified "Wild," 2 miles "Scenic," and 15 miles are classified as "Recreational." However you break it down, this is one great river. For a more expansive and in-depth description of the Chattooga, you may want to obtain a copy of *The Chattooga Wild and Scenic River* by Brian Boyd, published by Fern Creek Press (706) 782-5379.

Burrells Ford

Isolated crossing is a gateway to the northern Chattooga region

- **Hiking Trails**
- **Trout fishing**
- **Primitive campground**
- **Waterfalls**

A solitary fisherman below the bridge at Burrells Ford

To reach it from the Georgia side of the river requires a bumpy, winding 10 mile drive, but the bridge at Burrells Ford is one of only three bridges that span the Chattooga River between Georgia and South Carolina. Whether you enjoy hiking, camping or fishing, Burrells Ford is a great destination.

Though only about 15 miles downstream of its point of origin, the Chattooga at Burrells Ford has become a respectable mountain stream, averaging perhaps sixty feet or more in width. Burrells Ford makes an excellent starting point for both day and overnight hikers, as trails radiate in several directions.

Of particular note is the stunningly wild **Ellicott Rock Wilderness**, a 9,000+ acre preserve in Georgia and South Carolina established in 1975. Hikers heading north from Burrells Ford enter the Ellicott Rock Wilderness nearly immediately.

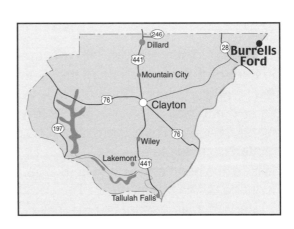

Hiking: Although the maintained trails around Burrells Ford are all located on the South Carolina side of the river, they are nearly always within sight of Georgia and Rabun County.

The best short hike is to pretty **King Creek Falls**, a cascading drop about 0.6 mile from the campground parking area. The trail to King Creek Falls begins in the upper corner of the parking area behind the information board.

North of Burrells Ford, a 3.8 mile section of the **Chattooga River Trail** leads to Ellicott Rock, the geographical point where Georgia, South Carolina and North Carolina meet. This section of trail closely follows the tumbling river. The first few hundred yards features a side trail leading to pretty **Spoon Auger Falls**, which occurs on a tiny tributary creek.

To the south, the **Chattooga River Trail** is a real wilderness adventure, stretching over 10 rugged miles to Russell bridge at Hwy. 28. About 7 miles south of Burrells Ford, the notable Bartram Trail intersects from the east. Notable sights on this section include **Big Bend Falls** (2.7 miles south of Burrells Ford) and **Licklog Falls**, adjacent to the **Bartram Trail** junction. In general, the scenery along the trail is magnificent, as steep forested riverbanks mingle with the ever-changing beauty of the Chattooga.

> Author's note: Be sure to obtain a topo map or the U.S. Forest Service map for the Chattooga River before hiking in this area. There are many rules and regulations which must be heeded, and the river corridor can become confusing to those not familiar with the area.

Camping: The campground at Burrells Ford is also located on the South Carolina side of the river. It is strictly primitive in nature, and requires a 350-yard walk to reach. A hand operated water pump and a pit toilet add a few touches of civilization, but otherwise you're on your own. The campsites are generally located close to the river, and several front tumbling King Creek as it rushes headlong to the Chattooga. There are also several riverside picnic tables here. The campground parking area is located 0.5 mile east of the Burrells Ford bridge.

Fishing: During peak periods in the trout fishing season, expect Burrells Ford to be crowded with anglers, both in the campground and in the river. Those who are looking for a quieter fishing experience will want to hike well upstream or downstream from the often crowded ford. Though the maintained trails are on the South Carolina side, primitive fishing paths extend both north and south on the Georgia side.

King Creek Falls
A short walk from Burrells Ford

Note: Be sure you possess a valid fishing license. Since the river is the boundary for between the two states, each state currently honors the other's fishing license and trout stamp.

Chattooga River Trail several miles north of Burrells Ford

Directions to Burrells Ford: From Russell bridge at Hwy. 28, proceed north (back into Georgia) on Hwy. 28 for 0.3 mile to the top of the first hill. Turn right onto FS 646 (Burrells Ford Road) and drive 10 miles to the ford. The main parking area is 0.5 mile beyond the bridge, (3 miles west of SC Hwy. 107).

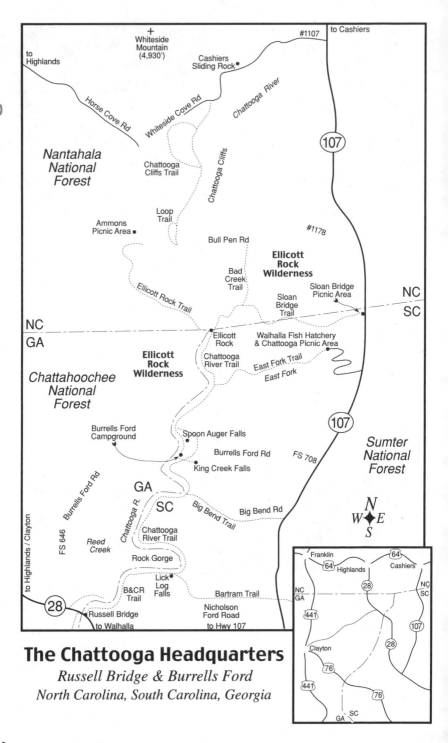

The Chattooga Headquarters
Russell Bridge & Burrells Ford
North Carolina, South Carolina, Georgia

Russell Bridge

Gateway region to Chattooga whitewater

- Hiking Trails
- Trout fishing
- Primitive camping
- Whitewater boating
- Historical exhibits

The West Fork flows peacefully below the Bartram/Chattooga River Trail footbridge.

Highway 28 crosses the Chattooga over Russell bridge, named for a pioneer family whose old 1800s farmstead lies about one mile east of the bridge. Russell bridge is located about 16 miles northeast of Clayton. Unlike most of the Chattooga watershed, much of the area south of the bridge comprises a surprisingly broad, gentle valley once utilized for agriculture. The river is quite tame as well, never raising its voice in either direction beyond relatively gentle shoals and small ledges.

Hiking: An abundance of trails and footpaths - among them the popular Bartram & Chattooga River Trails - combine to

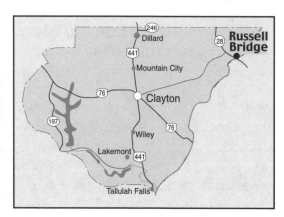

create an attractive destination for both hikers and fishermen. This area begs to be explored on foot. In addition to the trails, a veritable maze of old roads and primitive paths run alongside or near the river, eventually accessing some "special" area.

The **Bartram & Chattooga River Trail** crosses the river at Russell bridge and meanders south along the high riverbank on the Georgia side through a gentle, forested valley. This segment of the trail is easy to moderate, covering 20 miles before terminating at the next paved road - U.S. Hwy. 76 southeast of Clayton.

Dayhiking this portion of the trail is quite worthwhile, with gentle grades and beautiful scenery being the norm. About 0.25 mile south of Russell bridge, the trail crosses the West Fork of the Chattooga via a 120-foot long steel footbridge. Previously, hikers were forced to wade across the West Fork, an inconvenience at the least and a dangerous obstacle during periods of high water.

To the north, the **Bartram & Chattooga River Trail** utilizes the South Carolina side of the river, offering easy to moderate hiking for 4.8 miles up to several small waterfalls on Lick Log Creek. Here the Bartram Trail turns east and leaves the river corridor while the Chattooga River Trail continues north for approximately 6.7 miles up to Burrells Ford.

Reed Creek Bottoms and Gorge: This area makes a great destination for a 3-4 hour day hike, featuring the interesting Reed Creek area. The hike is easy to moderate, as long as you don't venture too far up the gorge. Hikes will probably range around 4-5 miles total. If you'd like to get off the "main" trails and do a bit of exploring, this could be a good option.

The easiest route to the bottoms is via an old gated logging road (FS 414) which meanders through a gentle forest of mixed hardwoods and white pines. The road intersects a wildlife clearing around mile 1.2. At the "special regulation" fishing sign, veer left onto a rugged path. This trail comes alongside the river just a few hundred yards beyond the wildlife clearing.

At mile 1.7 the trail enters the broad, flat flood plain (or bottoms, as locals call it) of Reed Creek. Much of this area was planted in loblolly pine years ago, and today is a mix of pine and hardwoods, with a heavy undergrowth of tall grasses.

The area along the river is still somewhat open, but quite overgrown with briars. Noisy Reed Creek, about 15-20 feet wide, flows along the eastern flank of the bottoms into the peaceful Chattooga. Several old trails knife through heavy underbrush and head north, passing through a stark stand of dead pines before following an old roadbed up to the mouth of the rugged Reed Creek gorge.

From here routes vary as the trails are fairly primitive and rough. Visitors possessing good backcountry skills can explore the gorge with caution. Numerous high shoals and small waterfalls lie interspersed along the steep, rocky creek. Several publications list a high waterfall a mile or so up the gorge, but reaching this goal would take considerable effort.

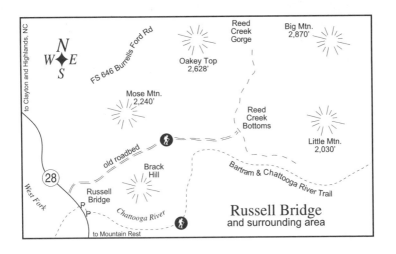

Russell Bridge
and surrounding area

An old roadbed runs alongside the river from the bottoms back to Russell bridge, but it has become so overgrown as to be practically useless as a means of transit. It would be wise to stick to the primary trails here, unless you like to duck and crawl through countless rhododendron thickets. If you want to explore the river along its banks, the South Carolina side of the river is a much better choice.

Be sure to take a close look at the pond behind the parking area at Russell bridge on the Georgia (west) side. This is a great spot to watch for wildlife.

Russell farmstead: Those with an interest in history will want to visit the old 1800s-era Russell farmstead, located just under a mile east of the bridge on Highway 28. An historical marker provides some interesting detail on these early settlers to this isolated South Carolina mountain valley, and the grassy strip along the highway features the remains of several outbuildings. The fields extending from the homestead out to the river are great places for a short walk. Be sure to explore the extensive "bamboo forest" along the river - kids love it!

Directions to Russell bridge: From the Days Inn in Clayton, turn east onto Warwoman Road and drive 13.7 miles to the stop sign at road's end. Turn right onto Hwy. 28 and proceed south for 2.2 miles to the roadside parking area preceeding Russell bridge. Another parking area is located on the South Carolina side of the bridge. This parking area is located adjacent to the trailhead for the Bartram & Chattooga River Trail.

Sandy Ford

A Chattooga River treasure amidst miles of hiking trails

- **Hiking Trails**
- **Fishing**
- **Waterfalls**
- **Whitewater boating**

Looking upstream from the beach at Sandy Ford

Sandy Ford is located about 3 river miles south of Earl's Ford, the major launching point for whitewater boaters floating beautiful Section III. This area is about 10 miles due east of Clayton.

Sandy Ford features a nice, wide beach formed as the river momentarily calms below a long series of challenging shoals. The Bartram and Chattooga River Trails access this area along the Georgia side of the river, and a short spur trail leads out to an impressive overlook at the brink of Dick's Creek Falls.

There is a whitewater boating access point across the river on the South Carolina side of the Chattooga, but the Georgia side is the better choice for hiking, camping (primitive only), wading and fishing due to the presence of the trail system. The beach on the Georgia side is a popular recreational spot.

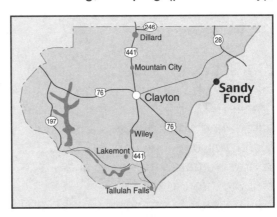

On the downside, Sandy Ford is the only location in the designated Wild and Scenic River corridor where visitors can drive their vehicles to the river's edge. Until the Forest Service and Rabun County can reach some type of agreement, vehicles on the beach (and sometimes even in the water) are commonplace in the warmer months.

Upstream from the beach and pool, the final drops of the Stairsteps, a lively Class 3 whitewater rapid, can be glimpsed. Two small islands split the river here, and several huge grey rocks jut outward from the sparkling riverbed.

Hiking: Both the **Chattooga River Trail** and the **Bartram Trail** cross Sandy Ford Road within a half-mile of the river, making numerous day hikes possible and allowing hikers to use Sandy Ford as a base for longer hikes. Sandy Ford is the mid-point of the riverside trail system between Russell bridge and Hwy. 76. In either direction the trail stretches 10 miles to these points. Just west of Sandy Ford a large roadside boulder inscribed "Bartram Trail" announces the trail crossing.

Just a few hundred yards east from this point is where the Bartram Trail intersects the Chattooga River Trail and the two become one as they wind north. From Sandy Ford Road the Bartram Trail winds west for 9 miles to Warwoman Dell near Clayton. Numerous publications detail the Bartram Trail's journey across Rabun County, while the Forest Service publishes an excellent map of the Chattooga corridor. Visit the U.S. Forest Service office on Hwy. 441 in Clayton to enquire about other resources.

Dick's Creek Falls: Dick's Creek Falls plunges into the majestic Chattooga River over a smooth mound of exposed granite. There are several possible routes that hikers may utilize, and none of them is particularly difficult, though a few of the trail junctions can be tricky. The shortest route possible is approximately 0.5 mile one way. Hazards include steep dropoffs around the falls.

The beauty of Dick's Creek Falls isn't the only attraction

here, as powerful Dick's Creek Ledge, a major Class 4 Chattooga rapid, surges at the base of the falls. The ledge occurs at a dramatic bend in the river where all the elements for a superb wilderness scene come together.

The waterfall has long been a familiar Chattooga River landmark to boaters, and hikers have made this a popular destination as well. Also known as "Five Finger Falls," due to the way the water divides into numerous tongues as it descends the rockface, a trip to Dick's Creek Falls offers one of the most dramatic vistas in Rabun County.

One route to the falls involves following the Bartram Trail north from Sandy Ford Road. It quickly intersects with the Chattooga River Trail. Continue about 0.5 mile north. Just beyond the point where the trail crosses Dick's Creek, turn right and follow the path downstream to the brink of the falls.

A second option involves parking your vehicle at the Dick's Creek ford on Sandy Ford Road. Follow the path on the north side of the creek for 200 yards. Cross the small branch and turn right. Walk down the old roadbed, which at times comes alongside scenic Dick's Creek. At 0.4 mile, the path crosses the Bartram & Chattooga River Trail before continuing several hundred yards downstream to the top of the waterfall.

Visiting here requires some good common sense. The rocks around the waterfall are smooth and slippery, and there are no railings to keep you away from the steep brink of the falls. Avoid the temptation to wade or swim in the river here - the current is powerful and foot entrapment is a very real possibility.

Dick's Creek Falls
aka Five Finger Falls

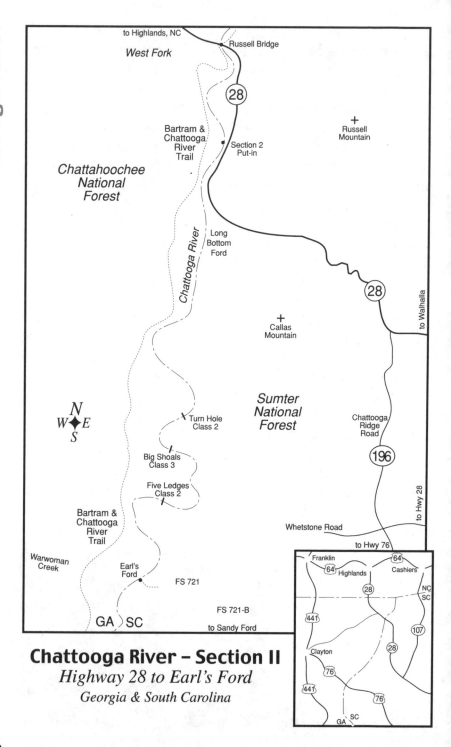

to Highlands, NC

Russell Bridge

West Fork

28

+
Russell
Mountain

Bartram &
Chattooga
River
Trail

Section 2
Put-in

*Chattahoochee
National
Forest*

Chattooga River

Long
Bottom
Ford

28

to Walhalla

+
Callas
Mountain

*Sumter
National
Forest*

Chattooga
Ridge
Road

N
W ◆ E
S

Turn Hole
Class 2

196

Big Shoals
Class 3

Five Ledges
Class 2

Bartram &
Chattooga
River
Trail

Whetstone Road

to Hwy 76

to Hwy 28

Warwoman
Creek

Earl's
Ford

FS 721

FS 721-B

GA SC

to Sandy Ford

Franklin

64

64

Highlands

Cashiers

28

NC
SC

441

107

28

Clayton

76

441

76

GA SC

Chattooga River – Section II
Highway 28 to Earl's Ford
Georgia & South Carolina

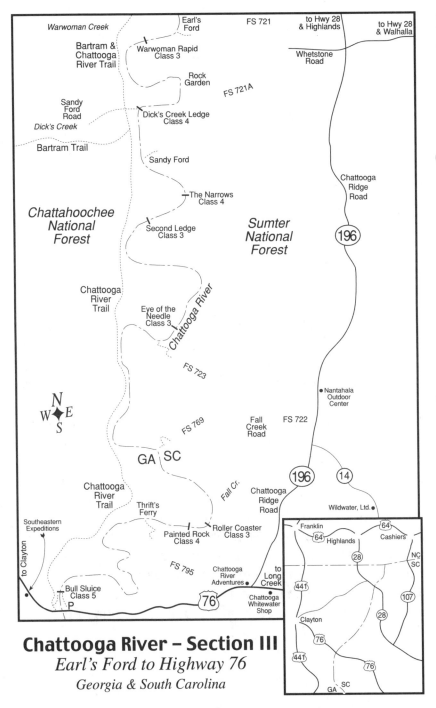

Chattooga River – Section III
Earl's Ford to Highway 76
Georgia & South Carolina

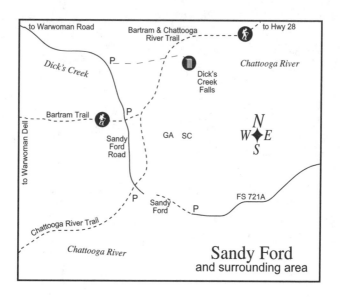

Sandy Ford
and surrounding area

Directions to Sandy Ford and the Dick's Creek Falls trailhead: From Hwy. 441 in Clayton, turn right onto Warwoman Road at the Days Inn and proceed 5.7 miles. Turn right onto Sandy Ford Road. Proceed 0.65 mile and turn left, crossing a bridge over Warwoman Creek. Drive 4 miles to the Dick's Creek ford.

If you want to hike the unmaintained trail to the falls, park here. To take the Bartram & Chattooga River Trail to the falls, continue on Sandy Ford Road *through the shallow creek* uphill to the Bartram Trail boulder about a quarter mile ahead. There is a small primitive parking area just before the trail crossing.

To reach Sandy Ford, continue another half mile past the Bartram Trail crossing. Be advised - the road beyond the trail crossing gets quite rough in certain spots and may not be suitable for passenger vehicles. In order to preserve the wilderness setting and protect the fragile riverside environment, please do not drive or park on the beach at Sandy Ford.

The U.S. Highway 76 Bridge

Major highway crossing provides a dramatic window on the river

Bull Sluice

- Hiking Trails
- Bull Sluice rapid
- Sandy beach
- Whitewater boating
- Fishing
- Info center

Note: This area becomes extremely crowded on warm weather weekends. Dangerous area – numerous swimmers have drowned here!

M any a visitor has first laid eyes on the legendary Chattooga River from the lofty perch of the Hwy. 76 bridge located about 9 miles southeast of Clayton. Besides being the closest river crossing to a populated area, a large parking area on the South Carolina side of the river provides easy access to Bull Sluice, a major Class 5 rapid, and a wide, sandy beach which serves as both a popular recreation spot and the major launching point for Section IV whitewater excursions.

Though the river is quite calm beneath the bridge, visitors only have to walk a few hundred yards upstream to witness a taste of the Chattooga's nasty side, as Bull Sluice is just upstream out of view.

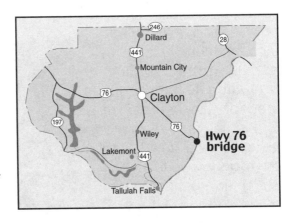

Trails head upstream along the riverbanks on both the South Carolina and Georgia side of the river. The path on the South Carolina side is both shorter and easier, but the Georgia path puts visitors directly atop the large rockpile above Bull Sluice. Take your pick, but be aware that the Georgia path requires much more energy to negotiate and can be dangerous if you choose to climb onto the rocks directly above the rapid.

The outstanding Chattooga River Trail currently ends here on the Georgia side of the bridge, though plans have been discussed which could extend the trail down to Tallulah Gorge State Park, approximately 10 river miles to the south. One historic feature worth mentioning is the remains of the old highway bridge skeleton, which still spans the river just a few yards from the modern structure.

Chattooga River Information Center: A large parking area on the South Carolina side of the river provides access to the beach and Bull Sluice via several short paths which originate from behind the information center. Here visitors may look over several Chattooga River exhibits explaining the wonders and dangers of the river. There are several pit toilets here as well, a real luxury along the river.

Trails to Bull Sluice: The paved path leading down to the beach is frequented by boaters carrying rafts, canoes and kayaks, while a short side path branching off to Bull Sluice has been graveled to handle heavy foot traffic. This trail is only a few hundred yards long, and terminates high above Bull Sluice, providing a panoramic view of this impressive Class 5 rapid. Many visitors climb down onto the rocks above the rapid, but be aware that slippery rocks and the extremely

A canoeist shoots the Bull

powerful current here makes this area quite hazardous, especially for children.

Bull Sluice is somewhat deceiving. First-time visitors may be disappointed in the rapid's appearance from afar, but rest assured that the drop looks much different from the inside of a canoe or raft as you negotiate this powerful monster. Spend a bit of time here in the prime boating months and you're sure to see some great wipe-outs.

The Georgia trail to Bull Sluice is about 0.4 mile long, and is moderate in difficulty. From the small parking area on the Georgia side of the bridge, follow the Chattooga River Trail north for several hundred yards, making a broad loop, then branch off to the right onto the old roadbed that begins a long descent down to the river.

Once at river level, you'll have to do a bit of scrambling over a number of rocks and downed trees which have been washed ashore. The trail passes one particularly interesting overhanging rock face before rock-hopping across rushing Pole Creek. Once across, choose your route to the top of the huge rockpile above Bull Sluice. This location provides a dramatic view straight down into the violent double drop, but exercise caution due to sheer drops and the powerful currents.

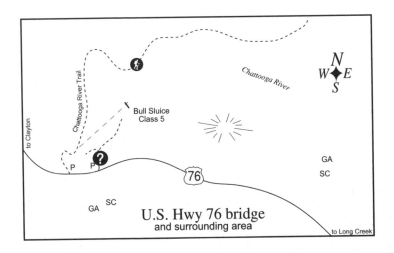

Chattooga River Trail

to Clayton

Chattooga River

N
W ◆ E
S

Bull Sluice
Class 5

GA
SC

P P

76

GA SC

U.S. Hwy 76 bridge
and surrounding area

to Long Creek

Chattooga River Trail

Great day or overnight hiking in the Chattooga River corridor

Looking downstream from the
base of Dick's Creek Falls.

- Hiking Trails
- Fishing
- Waterfalls
- Whitewater boating
- Primitive camping

Rabun County's portion of the **Chattooga River Trail** closely parallels the course of the river for 20 miles, from Hwy. 76 southeast of Clayton to Russell bridge at Hwy. 28. This is a beautiful wilderness trail, though its name is a bit of a misnomer. Only a limited portion of the Rabun County segment actually runs *alongside* the river. The vast majority of the trail stays within a quarter mile of the river within the protected river corridor, but does not offer the riverside experience one might expect from a trail associated with such a dramatic name. Because of its extended length and numerous access points, the trail offers excellent opportunities for day hikes and overnight trips.

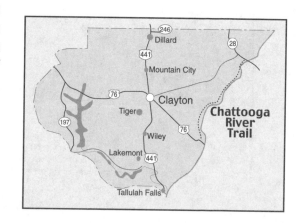

Russell bridge to Sandy Ford

Overview: This is a 10 mile section which features beautiful calm stretches of river, Dick's Creek Falls and numerous primitive camping spots. This segment is rated easy to moderate, and features a number of moderate uphill grades. Since both the **Bartram Trail** and the **Chattooga River Trail** are combined along this segment, there are portions where both the Bartram Trail's yellow diamond and the Chattooga River Trail's white blaze are present. As always, a detailed map is a good insurance policy. Note: This description is from north to south. See maps on pages 42 and 43.

General description: Russell bridge at Highway 28 marks the beginning of an enchanting 10 mile walk south to the Bartram & Chattooga River Trail split just west of Sandy Ford. This portion runs along the section of river known as Section II, widely recognized as the calmest of the river's three whitewater sections. Overall elevation changes are minimal along the trail, inviting hikers of all skill levels.

South of the Highway 28 bridge, the trail soon turns north and follows the West Fork of the Chattooga River up to a recently constructed bridge which stretches 120' across the river. Previously hikers were forced to ford the river on foot, which was hazardous at any time, and a dangerous obstacle during periods of high water.

The next 3 miles closely follow the river, often within a stone's throw of the scenic stream. Though the abundance of trees doesn't allow much of a long range view in the warm season, open views of the gentle valley in the winter are quite sublime. Boaters paddling along the placid river can be heard and seen along certain portions near the trail's northern end.

The valley narrows dramatically near its southern end, with the trail turning sharply west before crossing a small bridge over Adline Branch. The next 2 miles are moderately strenuous, with several moderate climbs and descents as the trail angles back into the Chattahoochee National Forest and away from the river. A crossing of scenic Laurel Branch marks the halfway point of this section as hikers negotiate a series of twisting turns along the base of 2,417' Willis Knob.

The path then begins a gradual descent to the east bank of Warwoman Creek, a major Chattooga River tributary. Just beyond Warwoman Creek is Earl's Ford Road, which not only provides access into the corridor but is a good emergency route off the trail. The trail parallels the creek for about 0.25 mile, then turns southwest toward the Chattooga River once again.

About one-half mile below Warwoman Creek, the trail intersects the river and closely follows it for the next 0.5 mile. Though the riverside scenery is not dramatic, this short section offers a welcome change for those who want to hike alongside the river. When the path angles away from the river again, hikers are in the vicinity of the "Rock Garden," a dramatic portion of the river which features giant slabs of rock extending from the riverbed. Refer to the U.S. Forest Service Chattooga River map for the exact location.

About 0.5 mile beyond, the trail crosses Dick's Creek, another beautiful tributary. Be sure to take the short walk down the spur trail alongside the creek to experience Dick's Creek Falls (see page 40) and massive Dick's Creek Ledge, a Class 4 whitewater rapid. All the dramatic elements of the river corridor come together here to create a vista that is not to be missed.

Continue south along the main trail for an additional 0.5 mile to the point where the trails split. Here the Bartram Trail turns and heads west toward Warwoman Dell, while the Chattooga River Trail continues south for an additional 10 miles to the U.S. Highway 76 bridge southeast of Clayton. The Bartram Trail crosses Sandy Ford Road just a few hundred yards from the junction, while the Chattooga River Trail crosses Sandy Ford Road about 0.4 mile south of the junction.

U.S. Hwy. 76 bridge to Sandy Ford

Overview: This 10 mile section features several miles of riverside hiking and boasts of a number of primitive riverside camping areas. This section of the trail is rated moderate. Note: This portion of the trail is described from south to north. See maps on pages 42 and 43.

General description: The southernmost section of the **Chattooga River Trail** winds 10 miles along a generally moderate grade from the heavy congestion of the Hwy. 76 bridge up to sparsely frequented Sandy Ford. This portion of the path travels closely along the river for less than 20% of its length, but it does afford a number of good spots to relax and explore once it comes alongside the river.

The trail originates in the small parking area on the northwest corner of the bridge, and follows white diamond-shaped blazes throughout its length. The initial 0.5 mile ascends gradually to a small footbridge over splashing Pole Creek. Once across, it proceeds along the steeply sloped and heavily wooded mountainside, far above the roaring Chattooga.

Several miles north of Hwy. 76, the trail begins a long, gradual descent which brings the hikers within close proximity to the river. This descent terminates after the trail crosses two small creeks. Shortly beyond, the trail turns sharply north and heads away from the river. It then begins a pulse-quickening climb of several hundred vertical feet along a low ridgeline just west of the Fall Creek junction. This portion of the trail shortcuts a wide bend in the river, trading a reduction in trail milage over riverside scenery. As the path descends from the ridge it intersects with the river at mile 5.5.

At this point, hikers who were looking for some Chattooga scenery can finally rejoice, as the next 1.5 miles closely follow the river. Here hikers have access to dozens of sandy beaches and numerous small, gurgling shoals. Although no major rapids are encountered, the overall scenery is outstanding, and several primitive camping areas are found along the trail.

At mile 7 the trail again leaves the riverbank and undulates through hilly terrain for the next several miles. Once again the path shortcuts a major bend in the river, only to drop again alongside the Chattooga across from Second Ledge, one of Section III's most exciting drops. Explore along the riverbank and you may find a good vantage point to watch boaters as they plunge over this dramatic 6-foot vertical ledge.

Beyond Second Ledge, the trail turns north and climbs from the river yet again. Several hundred yards beyond, picturesque Rock Creek is crossed. A short walk later, the trail crosses Sandy Ford Road. To the right, walk downhill along the road for several hundred yards to access the large beach at Sandy Ford.

Across the road, it is a 0.4 mile walk northwest to the junction with the **Bartram Trail**, which enters the river corridor via a 10 mile section originating in Warwoman Dell near Clayton. The combined trail, now known as the **Bartram & Chattooga River Trail**, continues north, winding 10 miles through the river corridor to Russell bridge and Highway 28.

The Lower Chattooga
Though difficult to access, the setting here is magnificent

- Dramatic scenery
- Hiking Trails
- Fishing
- Whitewater boating
- Primitive camping

A whitewater paddler drops into Jawbone rapid at Five Falls on the lower Chattooga

Rugged Section IV of the Chattooga River is located approximately 10 -12 miles southeast of Clayton. This is an area rich in natural beauty, but difficult to access. There are currently few established hiking trails in the lower river corridor on the Georgia side, but those pathways do access areas of tremendous beauty.

Raven Cliffs Trail: This pathway drops from a rugged Forest Service road down to a point on the river opposite massive Raven Cliffs. Raven's Chute, a Class 4 whitewater rapid, is located just upstream. This 0.8 mile trail is rated as moderate to strenuous due to a steep ascent.

Rugged Raven Cliffs is a very worthy destination

53

for those wishing to explore the Chattooga's legendary Section IV on foot. The hike isn't long or particularly difficult, the scenery is dramatic, and visitors are relatively few; all in all not a bad recipe for a short day hike.

The trail begins in a broad turnaround at the end of FS 511-B. The initial 0.6 mile follows an old logging road east towards the Chattooga gorge, gently descending through a mixed hardwood forest. A few white diamond blazes help to guide you here.

At 0.6 mile, the path begins a steep descent toward the river. Portions of the trail have been cut into the steep mountainside and reinforced with logs, creating a convenient manmade stairstep. Other stretches loop through broad, gentle switchbacks. Occasional glimpses of the river far below only serve to heighten the anticipation.

The trail terminates in a broad, flat knoll relatively clear of underbrush and frequented by untold numbers of campers over the years. A prominent fire ring has been arranged under large fragrant hemlocks and stately white pines, attesting to this location's popularity.

Just below this peaceful spot the Chattooga River pounds through a rock-strewn gorge beneath towering Raven Cliffs, a massive escarpment of broken grey rock arching over 100 feet above the surging river

A short boulder-hopping 100 yard scramble upstream along the Georgia bank provides visitors with a good view of Raven's Chute, a formidable river-wide ledge. Boaters normally run the ledge by hitting a narrow chute far across the river along the South Carolina

Rugged Raven Cliffs

bank. **Don't wade or swim here, as foot entrapment is a very real possibility. There have been boating and wading fatalities on this part of the river.**

Hikers can scramble up onto the ledge forming Raven's Chute and look far upriver to catch a glimpse of Deliverance Rock, a huge river-blocking boulder. While it is possible to hike along the river further upstream, heavy undergrowth and rugged terrain make this a venture only for the most hardened of outdoorsmen.

Directions to Raven Rock Trail: From the Hwy. 441 bridge in Tallulah Falls, head north for 3 miles and turn right onto Camp Creek Road. Proceed 2 miles to Water Gauge Road (FS 511 on the left). Follow FS 511 for 3 miles and turn left onto FS 511-B on the left. Follow FS 511-B for 0.8 mile until it deadends. The trail begins on the east end of the turnaround. Note: FS 511-B is rougher than FS 511, and has a few tricky areas to negotiate. If you are driving a normal passenger vehicle and the weather has been extremely wet, you may wish to walk the 0.8 mile to the trailhead and not risk getting stuck.

Camp Creek and Five Falls: These two destinations offer dramatically different adventures. The Camp Creek area is reached via a moderate quarter-mile trail from the parking area, and features a relatively placid stretch of river and picturesque Camp Creek. Five Falls, on the other hand, while only a half mile downstream, is difficult to reach as no maintained trail traverses the Georgia riverbank.

The Camp Creek Trail is really more of an access path than a real trail. The path begins at the base of a broad parking area and descends to the river in an area just upstream of the river's mightiest stretch of whitewater. A narrow strip of flat forest nestles against a stretch of the river aptly named, "the calm before the storm."

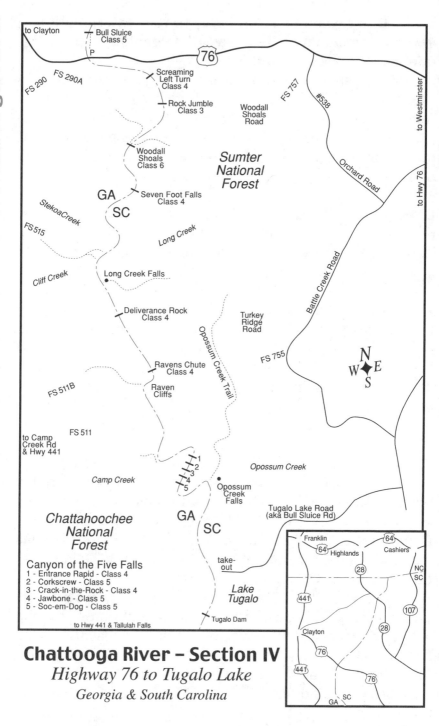

Chattooga River – Section IV
Highway 76 to Tugalo Lake
Georgia & South Carolina

Several small sandy beaches provide access to fishermen, boaters and hikers. Just downstream, lovely Camp Creek spills into the Chattooga. Several scenes from the motion picture "Deliverance" were filmed in this area, and the beautiful moss-covered rocks and fern splashed creekbanks create an enticing atmosphere.

Downstream of Camp Creek the river rounds a sharp bend and plunges into the legendary "Five Falls" section of the Chattooga. Here the river drops almost 75 vertical feet in a series of five back-to-back rapids. No discernible trail runs along the riverbanks, but Five Falls can be reached if you like to crawl, scramble and bushwack.

Another route to Five Falls roughly follows Camp Creek upstream. First, find the old roadbed that begins at the wooden footbridge along the riverside path that heads downstream to Camp Creek. Walk about 0.5 mile up this road. The path crosses Camp Creek and ascends south into a low gap. From here pick a desirable route back down to Five Falls. It's still not particularly easy or guaranteed safe, but those who don't mind hiking off-trail should be able to get there without too much problem. Be aware that the Five Falls area is very dangerous, with slippery rocks and numerous sheer drops. This is definitely not a place for children. The rewards are many, as dramatic views of boaters racing through rapids like Corkscrew, Jawbone and Soc-em-dog can be enjoyed from the (relative) safety of the riverbank.

The only other route into Five Falls is, unfortunately, not in Georgia. If you don't mind driving over into Long Creek, South Carolina, the Opossum Creek Trail will drop you onto the Chattooga riverbank about a half-mile downstream of Five Falls. If you really are passionate about hiking the Chattooga, both sides of the river are worth a visit.

Directions to Camp Creek: Follow the directions to the Raven Cliffs trail. Instead of turning left onto FS 511-B, continue straight ahead on FS-511 for another mile to its deadend (approximately 4 miles from Camp Creek Road).

Chattooga Boating Information

Dramatic whitewater and magnificent scenery

- Dramatic scenery
- Primitive camping
- Waterfalls
- Private boating and commercial trips

Note: See the back of this book for whitewater outfitters names and numbers.

A commercial rafting trip is the best bet for novices to experience the thrills and beauty of the Chattooga.

The Chattooga River features three excellent sections, each delightfully different. In general, the river becomes much more difficult as you head north to south, with Section IV being one of the most difficult whitewater runs in the eastern U.S.

The river is managed by the U.S. Forest Service, and they do enforce posted regulations. Regardless of the section you decide to attempt, **make sure you fill out the proper permits** (located at each put-in) **and observe all regulations. Numerous deaths have occurred on this river - it demands your respect.**

Section II

This is an excellent **7 mile** section featuring **easy to moderate whitewater** (numerous Class 2 rapids and one Class 3). Section II officially begins at Highway 28 (Russell bridge), but technically the put-in is located about a mile downstream of the bridge on the South Carolina side of the river.

This section offers a relatively calm trip down to Earl's Ford and the top of Section III. Only one major drop, Big Shoals (Class 3) is encountered, and it can be easily portaged if you are the least bit intimidated. The combination of easy access, forgiving rapids and outstanding scenery create an ideal beginners section while offering an enjoyable run for the more experienced boater as well. Whatever your mode of transportation - canoe, kayak, raft or innertube - Section II is a good choice. See map on page 42.

Section III

Section III is undoubtedly one of the most popular whitewater runs in the Southeast, offering **12.5 miles** of magnificent scenery and **moderate to advanced whitewater**. The river flows through the dramatic Chattooga River gorge from Earl's Ford to the Hwy. 76 bridge, plowing over dozens of exciting rapids, through mesmerizing rock gardens, and past beautiful stairstepping waterfalls.

Section III teases boaters with numerous Class 3-4 rapids and builds to a dramatic climax with the Class 5 Bull Sluice. In general, the current is much stronger and the rapids more numerous and technical than found on Section II. Paddlers should be of an intermediate to advanced skill level. Access through much of the corridor is difficult, so be sure of your paddling skills.

If you are a novice, one of the commercial outfitters is your best bet. Their safety record is outstanding, and they offer a variety of trips over different portions of Section III. The Section III map is on page 43, and commercial rafting companies are listed on page 124.

A beautiful portion of the Chattooga's Section III.

Section IV

As whitewater boating in the Southeast goes, this is as big as it gets. **Isolated, difficult and dangerous** are just a few of the modifiers commonly used to describe this portion of the river. Though only **7 miles long**, Section IV can require 4-8 hours to float due to extensive scouting required to run (or portage) these rapids.

Though the Chattooga is not a large river in terms of its overall volume, the intense drop-and-pool nature creates dramatic, and even legendary, whitewater. Many of the whitewater scenes in "Deliverance" were filmed on Section IV.

The average gradient per mile from the Hwy. 76 bridge to Lake Tugalo is a whopping **45 feet per mile**, making it one of the steepest whitewater runs in the east. Narrow rock-strewn gorges, sheer cliffs and wild waterfalls are only a taste of what you'll experience here. Boaters from across the country venture to Section IV to test this "experts only" whitewater. Never attempt this section unless you are a highly experienced, confident boater using all safety precautions. See Section IV map on page 80.

Though its reputation is primarily as a whitewater-only run, Section IV offers other attractions. Here a body–surfer enjoys a wild ride at Surfing Rapid.

For a more expansive and in-depth description of the Chattooga, you may want to obtain a copy of *"The Chattooga Wild and Scenic River"* by Brian Boyd published by Fern Creek Press (706) 782-5379.

Section Three

Recreational Destinations in the *Chattahoochee National Forest*

Southwest Rabun
- Fall Branch Trail — 62
- Joe Branch Trail — 64

Central Rabun
- Warwoman Dell Recreation Area — 66
- Falls on Martin Creek — 68
- Stonewall Biking Trails — 70

Northwest Rabun
- Coleman River Trail — 72
- Tate City and the upper Tallulah — 74
- Denton Branch Falls — 76
- Beech Creek Gorge — 77
- Appalachian Trail — 80
- Popcorn Overlook — 83
- Wildcat Creek — 84

Northeast Rabun
- Willis Knob Horse Trail & Camp — 85
- Holcomb Creek Trail — 86
- Rabun Bald — 88
- Three Forks — 91
- Bartram Trail — 94

Southwest Rabun
Fall Branch Trail
Easy, short stroll leads to beautiful Minnehaha Falls

- Scenic waterfall
- Short walk
- Primitive picnic spot
- Great photos

Note: Can become crowded on warm weather weekends!

The easy Fall Branch Trail terminates at the base of lovely Minnehaha Falls.

Spectacular Minnehaha Falls has long been known as one of Rabun County's most beautiful waterfalls. Though the trailhead can be a bit of a challenge to locate, the actual walk back to the falls is along an easy 0.3 mile trail just off Lake Rabun's heavily wooded southern shoreline. The term "Minnehaha" is Cherokee for "laughing waters," and as such is Rabun's most appropriately named cascade.

The path to the falls begins on the south side of isolated Bear Gap Road. The current trail marker is quite large and nearly impossible to miss, and is definitely an improvement over markers from earlier years which made locating the trailhead a bit of a guessing game. The initial one hundred yards of the path gradually climbs through a thick hillside grove of laurel and rhododendron which reaches a crescendo of color and fragrance in late spring and early summer. Far below the trail lively Fall Branch dances over a series of small shoals as it plunges toward beautiful Lake Rabun.

Other than a few steep dropoffs to the right and the usual nuisance roots and rocks, this trail is ideal for persons of any fitness level. Beyond the initial steps and incline, the trail levels for most of its length before making a short climb up to Minnehaha's base, where it ends at a flat grey rock slab just below the cascade's final drops.

This rock provides an excellent (and safe) observation point from which to enjoy the magnificent 60-foot waterfall as it stairsteps over a beautiful series of horizontal ledges. The upper cascades are particularly photogenic during the previously mentioned blooming season for laurel and rhododendron. Just downstream another set of cascades rushes among the streamside rhododendron. Though pretty, these cascades don't compare with Minnehaha's pristine beauty. Minnehaha Falls is a special place that is perfect for a short stroll or scenic streamside picnic - don't miss it.

Note: Do not climb this waterfall! The rocks are slippery and many injuries have occurred here!

Directions to Minnehaha Falls: From Tallulah Falls, drive north on Hwy. 441 for approximately 2 miles. Turn left onto Old Hwy. 441 (look for the Rabun Beach Recreation Area sign). Proceed 2.5 miles and turn left onto Lake Rabun Road. Proceed 6.2 miles.

Turn left onto Low Gap Road and proceed across the bridge over the Tallulah River. Proceed .15 mile up to the next stop sign. Bear left onto Bear Gap Road and drive 1.6 miles to the pull-off on the left.

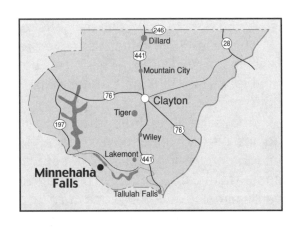

Joe Branch Trail

Pretty one mile hike leads to two scenic cascades

- Two pretty waterfalls
- Short walk
- Large camping area
- Convenient to Lake Rabun beaches, boating and fishing
- 700' elevation gain
- User fee required

Panther Falls, the first of two pretty cascades along the Joe Branch Trail

Joe Branch is a relatively unspectacular creek which just so happens to feature two very scenic cascades. A 1.2 mile trail (one way) originating in the Rabun Beach Recreation Area #2 campground heads north following the branch upstream into the steep watershed. This heavily shaded trail climbs gently through dense groves of streamside rhododendron past enormous oaks, poplars and fragrant hemlocks. Wildflowers are prevalent in season, but any time is a good time to tread this delightful path.

The initial 0.9 mile features several stream crossings before reaching pretty Panther Falls. This stairstepping 50-foot drop tumbles over an intricate series of ledges. The setting, while not dramatic, is still quite scenic.

Above Panther Falls the trail climbs steeply, brushing against the fall's uppermost cascades as it ascends ever deeper into the narrowing valley. The path is quite slippery in some spots - take care if you have children with you. Only about 600 yards remains until you reach the next destination, Angel Falls, but the distance may seem longer due to the increased steepness of the trail.

Angel Falls offers quite a different visual experience from Panther Falls, tumbling about 60 vertical feet over a wide, rugged rock face. Tiny Joe Branch loses much of its force as it fans out over the broad ledge, creating an intricate series of sparkling drops. The trail loops up to the base of the falls, allowing visitors to approach from either side, and a small platform at the base provides an excellent vantage point.

The Joe Branch watershed is quite small, and stream flow is critical to a "quality" waterfall experience here. If your visit is strictly to enjoy the waterfalls, you might avoid this trail during periods of prolonged dry weather. Since Rabun County normally enjoys generous rainfall year round, chances are you'll see some quality falling water. Even if the falls are lacking, the beauty of this area is always enchanting.

Directions to Joe Branch Trail: From Tallulah Falls, drive north on Hwy. 441 for approximately 2 miles. Turn left onto Old Hwy. 441 (look for the Rabun Beach Recreation Area sign). Proceed 2.5 miles and

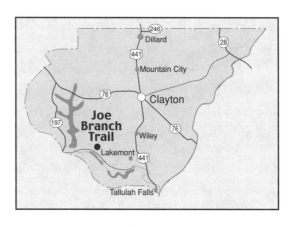

turn left onto Lake Rabun Road. Drive 4.5 miles to Rabun Beach Recreation Area #2. Proceed around the campground loop to the trailhead.

Central Rabun

Warwoman Dell Recreation Area

Delightful picnic area provides access to the Bartram Trail

- Becky Branch Falls is a short walk from the dell
- Picnic tables & pavilions
- Nature trail
- Historical remains
- User fee required

Rustic picnic shelter on splashing Becky Branch

Developed in the 1930s by the Civilian Conservation Corps and once used as a CCC camp, Warwoman Dell has been the site of a great deal of activity over the years. At one time this site actually housed an operational fish hatchery which provided trout for stocking on nearby creeks and rivers. Today picnickers and hikers frequent the peaceful, picturesque dell located just minutes east of Clayton on Warwoman Road.

Several picnic shelters and tables are scattered about the peaceful, secluded dell. An easy **0.4 mile nature loop** winds through the area, and the renowned Bartram Trail bisects Warwoman Dell as it climbs 13 miles north to Rabun Bald and 9 miles east to the Chattooga River.

Becky Branch Falls lies several hundred yards north of Warwoman Dell and the Bartram Trail passes within a few yards of this sparkling cascade. Just above the picnic area, remains of the ill-fated 19th century Blue Ridge Railroad run along the steep hillsides. An information board located in the upper end of the dell provides details for those interested in this fascinating yet failed project.

Becky Branch Falls: Typical of scores of cascades found on Rabun County streams, Becky Branch tumbles down a steep 20-foot rock face into a narrow ravine of dense hardwoods. Though only a short walk from the recreation area, the hike does require a steep uphill climb.

Visitors to Becky Branch Falls can almost reach out and touch the splashing waters from the relative safety of a conveniently positioned wooden footbrige spanning the creek. As is the case with many other local cascades, Becky Branch Falls occurs very high in its watershed, and therefore loses a great deal of spunk during dry spells.

Begin your hike at the first parking area on the left along the entrance road. Facing away from Warwoman Road, walk up the road and turn right onto the yellow-blazed Bartram Trail. The trail immediately passes the remains of the old fish hatchery before climbing to Warwoman Raod. Using extreme caution, cross the road and enter the woods via the clearly visible trail. Follow the path uphill toward the sound of falling water.

Directions to Warwoman Dell: From Hwy. 441 in Clayton, turn onto Warwoman Road at the Days Inn and proceed 2.4 miles to the Warwoman Dell Recreation Area on the right.

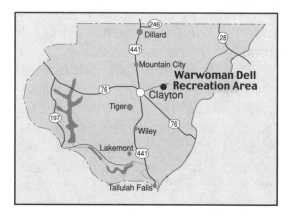

Central Rabun

Martin Creek Falls

Bartram Trail destination can be reached from Warwoman Dell

- Located along the Bartram Trail
- Moderate hike
- Several routes possible
- Highly scenic area

Note: the shortcut route requires walking off trail and can be confusing. It is always best to stay on an established trial.

The rugged 40-foot drop on Martin Creek is along the popular Bartram Trail.

A surprisingly scenic cascade on Martin Creek can be reached by walking an extra 30 minutes or so beyond Becky Branch Falls along the Bartram Trail. This powerful, two-tiered cascade drops into a shady, secluded grotto just off the famous trail.

There is a shortcut which cuts the walk down to about 0.4 mile (one way), but it involves parking at a primitive camping area along FS 152 and cutting through the woods. From the camping area (see directions on next page), locate the trail leading back into the woods. Veer right at the first fork, then rock-hop Martin Creek and head uphill along an overgrown path for about 200 yards up to the Bartram Trail.

Turn right and follow the Bartram Trail upstream for about 0.3 mile. The trail passes above a particularly powerful section of the creek that "flumes" down the narrow gorge. After passing an unusually scenic series of shoals and small falls, the path negotiates an area of open forest with several primitive campsites. Look for a wooden bridge spanning the creek and follow this side path up to an observation deck overlooking the waterfall.

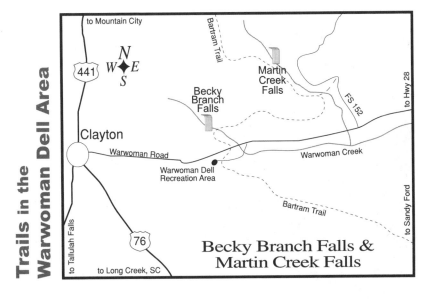

Becky Branch Falls & Martin Creek Falls

Directions to Martin Creek Falls: From Hwy. 441 in Clayton, turn onto Warwoman Road at the Days Inn and proceed 2.4 miles to the Warwoman Dell Recreation Area on the right.

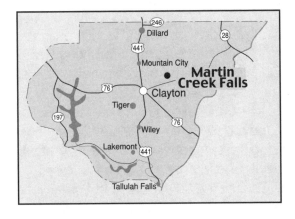

Take the Bartram Trail north for approximately 1.5 miles.

To reach the Finney Creek Road access point, continue down Warwoman Road an additional 0.7 mile beyond the dell, then turn left onto Finney Creek Road (FS 152). Drive 0.5 mile to a sharp left bend with a primitive camping area on the left. Park here.

Central Rabun
Stonewall Creek Biking Trails
Popular mountain biking trails feature plenty of action

- Twelve miles of challenging mountain bike trails
- Stonewall Falls
- Usage fee required

Note: recent power line construction has created confusion along portions of the Stonewall loop.

Pretty Stonewall Falls cascades into a broad pool alongside the popular Stonewall biking loop.

Known primarily for its pair of outstanding mountain bike trails, the Stonewall Creek area features plenty of outstanding scenery as well. In fact, those who don't care a lick about riding a bicycle through the rugged backwoods can still find something worthy to see here at Stonewall. While hiking is definitely not recommended on the biking trails (for obvious reasons), pretty Stonewall Falls is worth a visit, and is only a short walk from the parking area.

To visit the falls, park in the small lot adjacent to the start of the Stonewall loop. Walk downhill along the bumpy dirt road for about 0.4 mile. Stonewall Falls is located on pretty Stonewall Creek just a stone's throw from the bike loop. This cascade's 20-foot drop is surprisingly powerful at high water, and the broad pool below the falls is a popular swimming hole in the sweltering summer months. On the downside, a primitive camping spot is located adjacent to the falls, and litter can be a problem at this location.

Mountain Biking at Stonewall Creek

Stonewall Loop Trail: This **7.8 mile** trail has an overall elevation change of just under 500 feet. Those who know their mountain biking rate the trail as **moderate**. Advanced riders routinely traverse the trail in under one hour, while the "average" Joe tackles Stonewall in 1.5 to 2 hours. The riding surface is a combination of dirt roads (30%) and single track (50%), but recent power line construction has left portions of the roadway covered in loose gravel, creating a potentially hazardous ride.

Highlights of the loop include beautiful vistas from near the summit of Saga Mountain (elev. 2,260') and four, count 'em, *four*, crossings of broad Stonewall Creek. The trail passes Stonewall Falls just 0.4 mile before reaching the parking area.

White Twister Loop: Shorter and steeper than the Stonewall Loop, the White Twister is the newer of the two trails. This **4.2 mile loop** has an elevation change of about 350 vertical feet, and is generally considered **moderate to difficult**. The trail is steep in spots, and is overwhelmingly single track (approximately 98%). Bikers should be confident of their ability to remain in control under steep and challenging biking conditions.

Directions to Stonewall Creek: From Clayton, proceed south on Main Street (which turns into Old Hwy. 441) for 3.2 miles to the four-way stop sign in beautiful downtown Tiger. Continue south on Old 441 for 2.4 miles and turn right onto FS 20. Follow the gravel road for 1.6 miles and turn right into the small parking area.

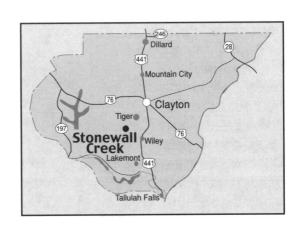

Northwest Rabun

Coleman River Trail

Beautiful mountain stream is a challenging trout destination

- **0.9 mile trail (one way)**
- **Pristine scenery**
- **Trout fishing**
- **Campgrounds nearby**
- **Usage fee required**

Note: Be sure to observe all posted regulations before fishing on Coleman River.

Three young hikers pause alongside one of Coleman River's cascades.

Scenic Coleman River is one of the upper Tallulah's major tributaries, and is an attractive destination both for hikers and trout anglers. To call Coleman a river is a bit of a stretch, but this lively ribbon of falling water has plenty to offer. An easy to moderate trail parallels the stream for nearly one mile northeast into the rugged watershed.

The trail climbs gently through an outstanding hardwood forest sprinkled with mature pines and shady hemlocks. The trail provides access to dozens of Coleman's small shoals and lively ledges. A few grades rate as moderately steep, but nothing too major. Riverside boulders provide some great picnic spots, and anglers will delight in the many deep pools along the stream.

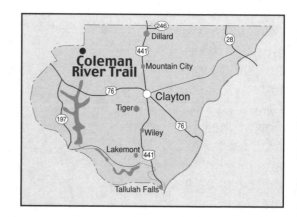

Directions to Coleman River: From Clayton, take Hwy. 76 west for 8 miles. Turn right onto Persimmon Road and proceed 4 miles to Tallulah River Road (FS 70) on the left. Follow FS 70 for 1.7 miles to the Coleman River bridge.

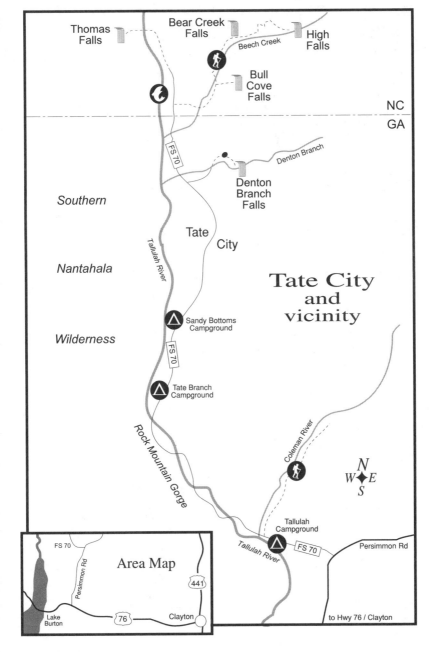

Northwest Rabun

Tate City and the upper Tallulah

Isolated valley is set amidst some of Rabun's grandest scenery

- Highly scenic drive
- Rock Mountain Gorge
- Trout fishing
- 3 Forest Service campgrounds
- See area map on page 73
- Usage fee required

Note: Use caution on FS 70 –
it is narrow and traffic is heavy
on warm weather weekends.

Simply put, Tate City and the upper Tallulah region is an area of superlatives. Here FS 70 closely hugs the rugged Tallulah River as it plunges through its steep northern watershed deep within the Southern Nantahala Wilderness. Campers can choose from 3 great U.S. Forest Service campgrounds located along FS 70, and both hikers and fishermen will find plenty to keep them occupied as well. In fact, the upper Tallulah is one of the region's premier destinations for trout anglers.

Tate City is as close as you'll come to civilization in these parts, and it isn't exactly the easiest place to get to. Though only about 12 miles by air from Clayton, the driving distance to Tate City is closer to 20 miles. Decades ago the area was home to a busy mining and logging industry that was far re-

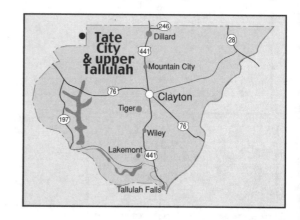

moved from civilization. Access into the upper Tallulah valley was difficult and time consuming, factors which ultimately ensured its survival in such a magnificent natural state.

One can't help but marvel at the rugged individualism that early settlers here must have exhibited. Today only a few dozen families make Tate City their home, though the population swells dramatically in the summer months when campers, fishermen and hikers flock to this dramatically beautiful setting.

Tate City and the upper Tallulah auto tour: The trip to Tate City and the upper Tallulah is worthwhile even if you never set foot outside of your automobile. Beginning at Persimmon Road, FS 70 heads north for 9 miles (most of it gravel), terminating about 2 miles north of the North Carolina line deep in the Southern Nantahala Wilderness.

The most dramatic portion of this drive is the 3 mile section of FS 70 directly alongside the plunging river in the dramatic Rock Mountain Gorge. This section of the roadway once held a narrow gauge railroad built to carry timber from logging operations around the Tate City area, and the roadbed was literally blasted into the steep mountainside. Keep your eyes open, as numerous streams cascade into the churning Tallulah from high above.

Beyond the gorge the road traverses the wide, peaceful valley known as Tate City. Home to farms, fields and a growing number of homes, Tate City is a stark contrast to the dramatic scenery of Rock Mountain Gorge.

North of Tate City the valley narrows once again and the road ends about 2 miles beyond the North Carolina line at a series of hiking trailheads.

The upper Tallulah drops wildly through the Rock Mountain Gorge along FS 70.

Northwest Rabun

Denton Branch Falls

It's a short walk to this pretty Tate City waterfall

- 0.4 mile walk (one way)
- Surprisingly powerful cascade
- Wilderness setting
- Rough .15 mile approach road
- See area map on page 73

Beautiful Denton Branch Falls plunges over a sheer ledge just minutes from Tate City.

While in the Tate City area, you might consider visiting pretty Denton Branch Falls. Follow the directions below to the creek ford, then carefully cross the creek on foot. Follow the old roadbed beyond the earthen mounds for about 0.2 mile.

When the road bends sharply left, bear right and follow another old roadbed which climbs moderately uphill for about 250 yards alongside Denton Branch. At the base of the falls, a small island is formed where the creek splits, providing an intimate view of this misty, surprisingly powerful 25-foot drop. It's somewhat overgrown and requires some rock-hopping, but Denton Branch Falls is a surprisingly scenic destination.

Directions: Take FS 70 for 6.6 miles to the unnamed dirt road on the right (the last dirt road before reaching the NC line). Drive approximately .15 mile to the parking pull-off preceding the creek crossing.

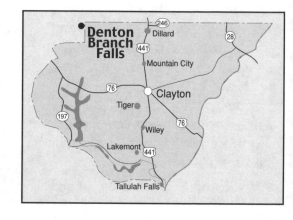

Beech Creek Trail – High Falls

Magnificent hike through a spectacular gorge

- 1 mile to Bull Cove Falls
- 2.4 miles to High Falls
- Moderate to strenuous hike – not for small children
- Numerous feeder trails
- Historic corundum mine in the area
- Trail can be overgrown in the warm summer months
- See area map on page 73

Distant Lake Burton as viewed from the Beech Creek Loop trail.

Don't tell anyone, but the Beech Creek gorge isn't in Rabun County. It is however, near the end of Tallulah River Road, and the only practical way to access this delightful path is by driving through Tate City...therefore it's in this guide. To put it briefly, this is why many people hike - waterfalls, wildflowers, beautiful wilderness setting, gorgeous vistas...well, you get the idea.

Experienced hikers love the Beech Creek area because it ties into several other trails, including the Appalachian Trail which crosses Standing Indian Mountain just a few miles to the north. There are any number of day and overnight hikes which can be staged from this area. For the purposes of this guide, only the 2.4 mile (one way) hike to High Falls will be detailed.

From the Beech Creek trailhead along FS 70, follow

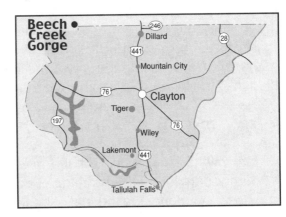

trail #378 into the woods. This trail gets your heart pumping from the start, as it makes a steep climb over Scaly Ridge. The path then descends the opposite side of the ridge and rock-hops across wide, splashing Beech Creek at mile 0.5. Several hundred feet beyond the trail intersects an old logging road. Turn left here and follow the roadbed for another 0.5 mile to where Bull Cove Creek flows across the road.

A red-blazed primitive path runs upstream along the north bank of Bull Cove Creek to your first Beech Creek Trail destination - **Bull Cove Falls**. This scenic 40-foot cascade is only about 100 yards from the main trail, but hikers can easily miss the spur trail unless they are looking for it. Bull Cove Falls is worth the diversion, as it plummets in several stages into a narrow, rocky cove.

Rocky grotto and lower cascades of Bull Cove Falls.

Beyond Bull Cove Creek, the Beech Creek Trail retains a gentle grade before fording Beech Creek and entering the Beech Creek gorge. The going gets a bit tougher here, as the path begins a steady, unrelenting climb over the next several miles as it ascends into the steepening gorge.

About 0.4 mile beyond the Beech Creek ford, Bear Creek Falls can be glimpsed high above the trail on the steep mountainside. Far below the falls the creek runs across the trail before merging with Beech Creek. This waterfall consists primarily of a series of steep waterslides, most of which are hidden in the foliage high above the trail. This particular portion of the path features several small cascades which occur on feeder creeks. Those with a keen eye can view a number of these falls, but most are, once again, well hidden by heavy undergrowth, especially in the warmer months of the year.

At about mile 2.0 the remains of corundum mining activity can be found alongside the trial. These historic remains signal the beginning of a series of switchbacks which ascend the southeastern flanks of Big Scaly Mountain. Proceed to the beginning of the second switchback to the left and a small sign (normally present) will direct you onto a narrow side trail which descends several hundred yards to the base of magnificent **High Falls**.

Those who have endured to this point are rewarded with an incredibly beautiful wilderness waterfall which relatively few visitors get to enjoy. Here in the splendid isolation of the Beech Creek gorge High Falls splashes over a rugged cliff which reaches approximately 100 feet up the steep mountainside.

If this is the end of your trip, be sure to enjoy every step of the return journey through this beautiful wilderness setting. Consult other hiking guides concerning longer trips in this

The author enjoys a dramatic view of magnificent High Falls.

area. The entire Beech Creek loop requires about 7 miles of serious hiking, but destinations such as the Beech Creek flats, the summit of Big Scaly Mountain and Chimney Rock make this area well worth the effort. If the hike to High Falls isn't much of a challenge, take a closer look at the entire Beech Creek loop at some point in the future.

Directions to the Beech Creek Trail: From Persimmon Road, follow FS 70 for 7.8 miles (about 0.4 mile past the NC line). Look for the Beech Creek Trail marker on the right. Either park across the road in the clearing or drive to the end of FS 70, park, then hike back down to the trailhead. Note: The end of FS 70 serves as the upper trailhead for the entire 12 mile Beech Creek loop. If the gorge and waterfalls are your destination do not access the trail from the northern end.

Northwest Rabun
Appalachian Trail
Over eight miles of this historic pathway straddles the Rabun line

- Beautiful vistas
- 16.6 mile section from Unicoi Gap to Dick's Creek Gap
- Moderate to strenuous
- Wilderness backcountry

Typical of the vistas visible from the Appalachian Trail in Rabun County.

Many of Rabun County's trails lead alongside beautiful rivers or streams or terminate at spectacular destinations such as waterfalls. Some, like the Bartram or Appalachian Trails, simply pass through the area as a small portion of a much longer trail. Rabun County hosts about 8.4 miles of the legendary AT.

As it climbs northward toward the rugged Nantahala Mountains the AT hugs the Rabun/Towns County border along a seemingly endless series of peaks and gaps - from just north of Tray Mountain on the southern end to near Rocky Knob near the North Carolina line. In fact, this section is quite representative of much of the 2,100 mile trail that runs from Georgia's Springer Mountain to Mt. Katahdin in Maine.

Elevations along this 16.6 mile section range from 2,675' in Dick's Creek Gap to 4,430' atop Tray Mountain. Needless to say, elevation changes of this magnitude make for an exhilarating hiking experience. Only those in excellent physical condition should attempt this portion of the AT.

General trail description: The 16.6 mile segment from Unicoi Gap to Dick's Creek Gap is often referred to as Section 5. Several miles of Section 6, which heads north from Dick's Creek

Gap toward the North Carolina line, also travels through a small portion of Rabun. For a more thorough description of either section, consult one of the many good AT guidebooks. Casual visitors looking for a short AT day hike should be able to tackle a few miles either north or south from Dick's Creek Gap with no problems.

Section 5 makes an ideal 2 day hike, with primitive camping sites and water sources both readily accessible. One of the better water sources is at mile 5.5, where a side trail winds down to a spring and shelter. The views are excellent along this section, particularly from the rocky top of Tray Mountain. Tray is the second highest AT summit in Georgia, and the panoramas from atop this wilderness peak are among the best in the Georgia mountains.

The 5.8 mile segment stretching from Tray Mountain to Addis Gap cuts through the heart of the 10,400-acre Tray Mountain Wilderness. Next up is a 5.4 mile section from Addis Gap to Dick's Creek Gap. This segment closely parallels the dividing line between two vast game management areas - the 19,000 acre Swallow Creek Wildlife Management Area to the west, and the 12,600-acre Burton WMA to the east.

Directions to both trailheads: The Unicoi Gap trailhead is located 9 miles north of Helen on Hwy. 17-75. Dick's Creek Gap is located on Hwy. 76 approx-imately 16 miles west of Clayton. Be sure to lock your vehicles and keep anything of value out of sight. Vehicle security is an issue at any isolated trailhead.

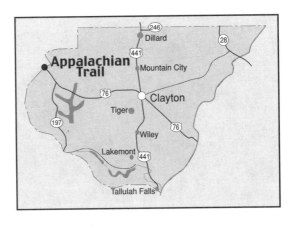

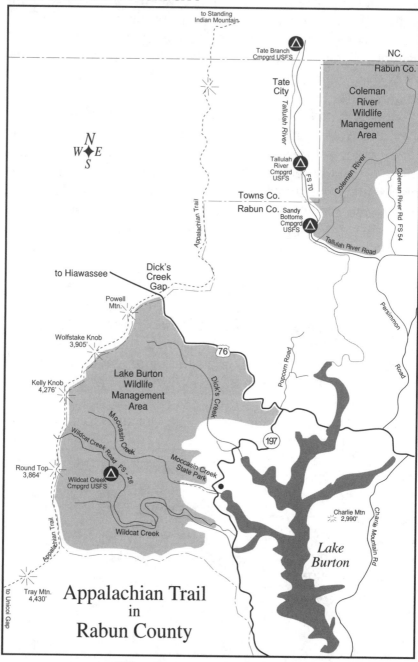

to Standing
Indian Mountain

Tate Branch
Cmpgrd USFS

NC.

Rabun Co.

Tate
City

Coleman
River
Wildlife
Management
Area

Tallulah River

Coleman River

Coleman River Rd FS 54

N
W◆E
S

Appalachian Trail

Tallulah
River
Cmpgrd
USFS

FS 70

Towns Co.

Rabun Co.

Sandy
Bottoms
Cmpgrd
USFS

Tallulah River Road

to Hiawassee

Dick's
Creek
Gap

Persimmon Road

Powell
Mtn.

76

Wolfstake Knob
3,905'

Lake Burton
Wildlife
Management
Area

Popcorn Road

Dick's Creek

Kelly Knob
4,276'

Wildcat Creek Road FS - 26

Moccasin Creek

197

Round Top
3,864'

Wildcat Creek
Cmpgrd USFS

Moccasin Creek
State Park

Charlie Mtn
2,990'

Wildcat Creek

Charlie Mountain Rd

Appalachian Trail

Lake
Burton

Tray Mtn.
4,430'

to Unicoi Gap

Appalachian Trail
in
Rabun County

The Appalachian Trail
from Tray Mountain to the North Carolina state line

Popcorn Overlook

Beautiful vistas north into the Southern Nantahala Wilderness

- **Scenic overlook**
- **Picnic tables**
- **Appalachian Trail nearby**

Morning fog fills the valley as the sun rises at Popcorn Overlook.

The thirty-mile segment of Highway 76 that runs from Clayton to Hiawassee features a splendid diversity of beautiful mountain scenery. While the initial one-third traverses a string of peaceful valleys between Clayton and Lake Burton, the middle third climbs well up into the mountains between the lake and the AT junction at Dick's Creek Gap.

Several miles prior to reaching the AT, the highway passes scenic Popcorn Overlook, a north-facing pull-off with magnificent views into North Carolina's Southern Nantahala Wilderness. The unusual name comes from a nearby trout stream. Popcorn Overlook is nice but definitely no frills. A few picnic tables and a great view is all you'll find.

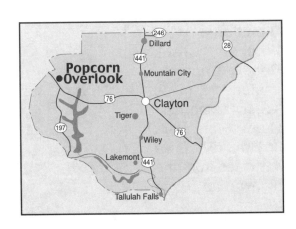

Directions:

Popcorn Overlook is located 12 miles west of Clayton on Hwy. 76.

Northwest Rabun

Wildcat Creek

Anglers, campers and sightseers enjoy Wildcat's beauty

- **Beautiful streamside scenery**
- **Trout fishing**
- **Sliding Rock**
- **Forest Service campgrounds**
- **Usage fee required**

Sliding Rock on Wildcat Creek.

Known primarily as a prime trout fishing stream, beautiful Wildcat Creek offers up plenty of scenery to visitors travelling along West Wildcat Creek Road (FS 26) just west of Lake Burton. The first several miles of FS 26 closely parallel the rushing creek. This section features scores of small falls and sparkling cascades.

Though fishermen rule the area during trout season, one spot, known as Sliding Rock, attracts swimmers who brave frigid waters to race down the steep 6-foot rock face into a broad plunge pool. Two U.S. Forest Service primitive campgrounds are located further up FS 26. The road offers plenty of good scenery, terminating 8 miles in from Hwy. 197.

Directions: West Wildcat Creek Road is approximately 1.5 miles south of Moccasin Creek State Park on Hwy. 197. Drive 1.4 miles from the highway to reach Sliding Rock.

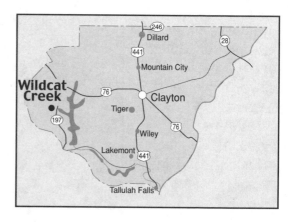

Willis Knob Horse Trail

Riding trails and camps span the Chattooga River

- **Nearly 30 miles of riding trails**
- **Willis Knob camp in Georgia**
- **Whetstone camp in South Carolina**
- **Brochure available from USFS in Clayton**
- **Fees required for camp usage**

Georgia's Willis Knob Horse Trail and South Carolina's Rocky Gap Horse Trail offer riding enthusiasts nearly 30 miles of scenic horseback riding. Connected by three Chattooga River fords, these two trail systems boast beautiful scenery from two national forests, the Chattahoochee in Rabun County and the Sumter in Oconee County, SC.

What's a system of extended trails without a camp? Both sides of the river feature excellent horse camps. The Willis Knob Horse Camp on the Georgia side features nine sites that are available by reservation only (go online at reserveamerica.com) or call toll free 1-(877) 444-6777. The Whetstone horse camp has several sites that can be reserved. Unreserved sites are on a first-come basis. Call (864) 638-9568 for details.

Directions: From Clayton, turn east onto Warwoman Road at the Days Inn and drive 11.6 miles. Turn right onto Goldmine Road (FS 157) and proceed to the day use area or camp.

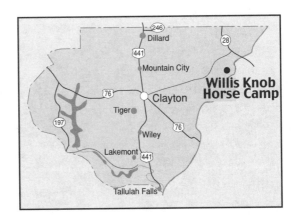

Northeast Rabun
Holcomb Creek Trail
Two scenic waterfalls in a beautiful wilderness setting

- **Two pretty cascades**
- **Short hike**
- **Isolated wilderness setting**
- **Alternate trailheads provide several hiking options**

Rhododendrons in full bloom frame a mist–shrouded Holcomb Creek Falls.

One of Rabun County's better known wilderness waterfalls actually gives you two for the price of one. This destination is the scenic Holcomb Creek Trail and a short walk here provides a closeup view of two very different cascades on neighboring creeks.

From the trailhead at the intersection of FS 7 and FS 86, follow the shady path as it descends into the forest. After only 0.3 mile magnificent Holcomb Creek Falls appears around a bend in the trail. This beautifu stairstepping waterfall descends approximately 120 feet. The upper cascades free-fall over a series of ledges, while the lower portion slides over a steep rock face. A footbridge at the base of the falls provides a perfect vantage

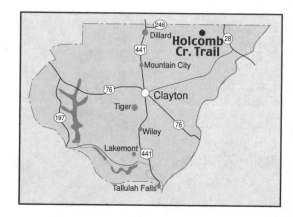

point. Please resist the urge to climb the rocks around the base as they are extremely slick. Numerous accidents have occurred here over the years.

Beyond Holcomb Creek the trail climbs moderately for several hundred yards. Shortly after passing a spur trail to the left, the path terminates at pretty Ammons Creek Falls (also known as Emory Falls). Ammons Creek Falls spills over a steep rocky ledge adjacent to a large wooden observation deck. Though not nearly as scenic as Holcomb Creek Falls, the cascade is nonetheless worth a look.

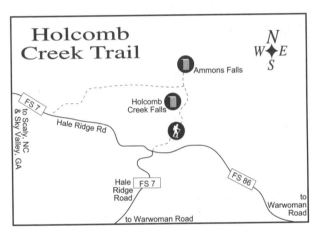

On the return trip, hikers may either retrace their steps back to the original trailhead or opt to take the spur trail back out to Hale Ridge Road. This alternate trail runs about one mile upstream along Holcomb Creek to an alternate trailhead about 0.6 mile up the road from the original trailhead. Those who opt to hike this spur trail need to know that it includes a pretty significant uphill stretch.

A quick in-and-out to Holcomb Creek Falls gives you a walk of around 0.6 mile. If you opt to visit both falls and return via the spur trail and road, you'll travel just over 2 miles.

Directions: From the Days Inn on Hwy. 441 in Clayton, take Warwoman Road east for 9.7 miles. Turn left onto Hale Ridge Road (FS 7) and drive 6.6 miles to the intersection of Hale Ridge Road and Overflow Road. The lower trailhead is located on the north side of the intersection.

Northeast Rabun
Rabun Bald
Spectacular panorama from atop Georgia's second highest peak

- **Tremendous views**
- **Numerous hiking options**
- **1.7 miles (one way) from Bee Gum Gap**
- **0.7 mile (one way) from access road turnaround**

The old observation tower atop Rabun Bald.

Massive Rabun Bald guards Georgia's northeastern corner, and at a lofty 4,696' this peak is officially the state's second highest. Rabun Bald offers a refreshingly different experience from the crowds and development atop Brasstown Bald, Georgia's highest peak. The lack of facilities and elusive trailheads make this summit one of Georgia's wildest locations.

Several routes to the summit are available. A spur trail leads from Bee Gum Gap to the Bartram Trail, creating a 1.7 mile summit trek which ascends approximately 1,000 vertical feet. Another choice is easier, sort of. This route requires visitors to drive (or walk) up the bumpy, 1 mile access road that accesses a tiny parking area about 0.7 mile below the summit. Be advised this "road" is

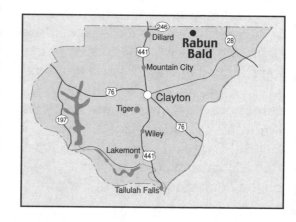

absolutely unsuitable for anything other than 4WD vehicles. The Bartram Trail intersects the access road at a small turnaround before continuing its climb to the summit. The trail switchbacks through a dense grove of rhododendron and laurel before flattening out as it attains the summit ridgeline.

The dense vegetation thins greatly on the windswept summit, where a grand decades-old stone tower with a wooden observation deck rises above the treeline, offering a magnificent 360-degree view. When visibility permits, distant peaks in the Great Smoky Mountains are visible. To the north and west are the rugged summits of the Nantahalas. To the south and east a series of ridges fades into the horizon, and the piedmont region of South Carolina is plainly visible. This is a wonderful spot to linger; if you're into great views, it just doesn't get much better than the lofty summit of Rabun Bald.

Several other challenging hiking trails are accessible from atop Rabun Bald. The steep **Three Forks Trail** drops from the summit down to Hale Ridge Road (3 miles one way) before turning east and heading an additional 6 miles out to the West Fork of the Chattooga River. The renowned **Bartram Trail** stretches north from the summit to Hale Ridge Road and south to Warwoman Dell, a distance of 14.5 miles.

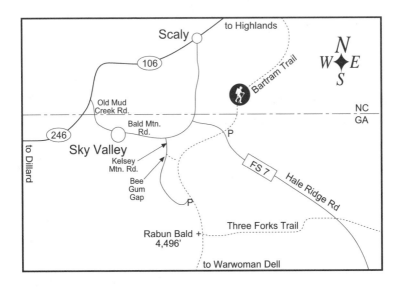

The dramatic panorama to the north from the Rabun Bald tower.

Directions: From Dillard, take GA 246 for 4.3 miles. Turn right onto Old Mud Creek Road at the Sinclair gas station. Proceed 2.8 miles. Turn right onto Kelsey Mountain Road (there should be a USFS Rabun Bald sign here). Proceed 0.3 mile into Bee Gum Gap. At the end of the pavement continue straight ahead, bearing slightly right onto the primitive roadway which climbs to the upper parking area.

Note: This "road" actually may provide the best walking route to the summit. *This road has the potential to damage even good 4WD vehicles*. You may want to park in the gap (careful to stay off private property and not block any drives) and walk up the road or take the spur trail over to the Bartram Trail and continue up from there.

The least confusing and best pure hiking route is to drive down Hale Ridge Road (FS 7) and hike the Bartram Trail all the way to the summit.

Three Forks
Rugged backcountry destination is a challenge to reach

- Wilderness setting
- Outstanding scenery
- Waterfalls
- Trout fishing
- Not suitable for children

The rugged West Fork of the Chattooga River at Three Forks.

The Three Forks Trail is one of the more challenging pathways in Rabun County. Originating high atop Rabun Bald, the trail drops several thousand feet in elevation in its 9+ mile journey down to Three Forks, the birthplace of the West Fork of the Chattooga River.

The name of the trail is a bit of a misnomer, as the "official" portion of the Three Forks Trail has historically ended about a half-mile from Three Forks proper. While the bulk of the trail features great hiking and beautiful scenery, Three Forks, with its splendid scenery, isolation and abundant wildlife, is a wilderness destination worthy of special mention.

Novice hikers may wish to tackle the one mile hike (one way) from John Teague Gap to the small, powerful cascade on Holcomb Creek upstream of Three Forks. This white-blazed trail meanders along a high, dry ridge featuring broad vistas to the north.

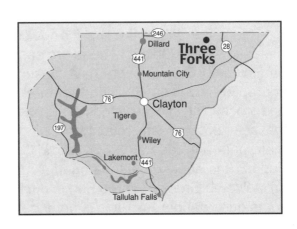

91

Far below, Holcomb Creek softly serenades hikers as its waters roar through a rugged gorge. Approximately 1 mile from the trailhead the path drops down onto an old logging road.

To reach the small falls on Holcomb Creek, turn left here and follow the rutted road down toward the sound of rushing water. The trail ends on a large rock perched above a powerful fluming cascade. Note the potholes carved into the solid rock by the powerful swirling currents of Holcomb Creek. Use extreme caution here - this is a dangerous area. Upstream numerous small cascades intersperse with calm, clear pools frequented by trout fishermen.

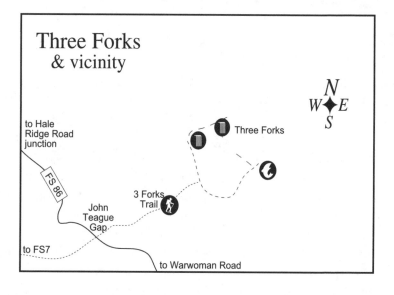

This is the end of the line for novices. There are several routes to Three Forks, but none are easy. From the small falls on Holcomb Creek, hikers have basically two choices. The first option involves crossing the creek (well above the falls) and proceeding into the woods along one of the primitive "paths" that head downstream, roughly following Holcomb Creek. The main path emerges along Overflow Creek just above Three Forks. It is approximately a quarter-mile from the small falls on Holcomb Creek to Three Forks, but it is steep, and in a few spots quite dangerous - this is not a destination for children!

Despite the challenges and frustrations, Three Forks is a very worthy destination. Here the mighty West Fork is formed by the near right-angle confluence of Big Creek, Overflow Creek and Holcomb Creek. Holcomb and Big Creek enter the junction over small, sparkling waterfalls. Overflow Creek features its own cascade, but it is located well upstream. Other large falls are located on Big Creek but they require a considerable hike upstream to reach.

Three Forks offers an imposing wilderness setting with mammoth boulders and sheer bluffs perched above the rushing stream. Movement along the riverbank is somewhat slow and frustrating, but for those who want to explore in a dramatic wilderness setting, Three Forks is a great destination.

Another path originates back at the point where the trail and old logging road intersect about 1 mile from the original trailhead. Follow the roadbed uphill to the primitive campsite. Turn right and follow the well-worn path beyond the vehicle-blocking mounds and proceed about 0.4 mile down to the West Fork. The last few hundred yards is extremely steep and potentially dangerous. This portion of the West Fork is absolutely beautiful. Though only a few hundred yards downstream of Three Forks, it is a dangerous and difficult journey upstream and really not practical for anyone but the hardiest of adventurers.

Note: It is highly recommended that anyone visiting Three Forks carry a copy of the USGS topo map for this area. Carrying a GPS device is also a good idea. It would not be difficult to get turned around in such a rugged backcountry area. Use extreme caution here - in the event of an accident help would be a long time arriving.

Directions to the Three Forks trailhead: From Clayton, turn onto Warwoman Road at the Days Inn. Drive 13.5 miles and turn left onto Overflow Creek Road (FS 86) just beyond the West Fork bridge. Proceed 4 miles to John Teague Gap. There is a small parking area here. The trailhead to Three Forks is on the right (northeast) side of the road.

Northeast Rabun

The Bartram Trail

Retracing the path of 18th century naturalist William Bartram

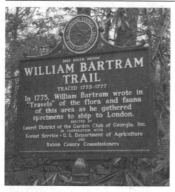

- **37 total miles in Rabun County**
- **Trail ranges from rugged summits to riverside scenery**
- **Easy to strenuous, depending on segment hiked**
- **Wilderness camping**
- **Yellow–blazed trail**
- **Obtain a detailed map/guide**

Bartram Trail marker at Warwoman Dell.

Rabun County's longest single trail roughly retraces 18th century explorer and naturalist William Bartram's travels through the Rabun County region around 1775. Bartram's extensive descriptions of his explorations helped guide modern day explorers to closely retrace his journey through the development of a trail named in his honor. Thirty-seven miles of this impressive trail loop through Rabun County's northeast corner, offering hikers a tremendous outdoor experience.

Rabun's portion of the Bartram Trail begins on the North Carolina line just south of Osage Mountain. The trail climbs east of Sky Valley up to the summit of Rabun Bald, then begins a gradual descent over a series of peaks and gaps down to Warwoman Dell, nearly 14 miles distant.

Turning east, the trail heads over

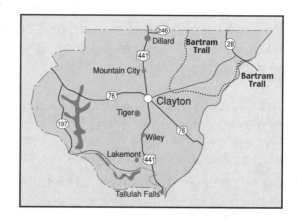

a series of low ridges for 9 miles out to Sandy Ford Road and the Chattooga River. Here it merges with the Chattooga River Trail and turns north, closely following the river for 10 scenic miles up to Highway 28. The trail crosses into South Carolina over Russell bridge and continues north.

Hale Ridge Road to Warwoman Dell

This 17.5 mile segment is rated as moderate to strenuous, and is definitely the most challenging Bartram section in Rabun County. This portion of the Bartram Trail mimics the personality of the nearby Appalachian Trail as it traverses a seemingly endless string of alternating peaks and gaps. If you hate flat ground, this is the trail for you - it's a real calorie burner.

Elevation readings reflect the type of hike you can expect as you move from north to south: 3,280' at Hale Ridge Road; 3,640' at Bee Gum Gap; 4,696' atop Rabun Bald; 3,740' at Salt Rock Gap; 4,100' atop Flat Top; 3,260' at Rock Mountain Gap; 3,690' at Rock Mountain; 1,920' at Warwoman Dell.

In general the trail is well constructed and the yellow blazes easy to follow. The path utilizes dirt or gravel roads along several short sections, and hikers must pay close attention to blazes and signs to keep from getting off the trail.

The highlight of this section is undoubtedly the panorama from atop massive Rabun Bald. This 360-degree view from atop the old stone tower is one of the best in the southern Appalachians. Several other excellent vantage points include overlooks at Wilson Knob and Double Knob. Two small cascading falls occur in the final two miles: a rushing 40' waterfall on Martin Creek and pretty Becky Branch Falls just a few hundred yards north of Warwoman Dell.

Warwoman Dell to Sandy Ford Road

The middle segment of Rabun's Bartram Trail meanders east for 9.4 miles from Warwoman Dell Recreation Area near Clayton to a junction with the Chattooga River Trail just west of Sandy Ford. While there is still quite a bit of climbing and descending, the elevation changes on this section are more moderate and therefore the trail is more suitable for novice hikers. The forest is still quite beautiful with several spots offering limited vistas of the surrounding peaks. The trail crosses Pool Creek Road at mile 5.9, allowing the hike to be broken down into smaller segments.

Hikers looking for a spot to camp along the Bartram Trail have many options to consider. Literally dozens of good camping sites are available, most featuring old fire rings offering mute testimony to the scores of visitors who have enjoyed this portion of the trail over the years.

The trail crosses Sandy Ford Road just a few hundred yards west of its junction with the Chattooga River Trail. A large inscribed boulder marks the crossing and a small pull-off just up the road provides a location to park your vehicle.

Sandy Ford Road to Highway 28 (Russell Bridge)

The final leg of the Bartram's journey through Rabun County is an easy to moderate 9.8 mile leg which traverses the Chattooga River corridor from Sandy Ford north to Highway 28. This portion of the trail combines with the Chattooga River Trail, and is described in more detail on pages 49-50.

Chattooga River below Dick's Creek ledge just a short walk from the Bartram Trail.

Though the trail spends more time deep in the forest than along the scenic riverbanks, highlights include the spur trail leading out to dramatic Dick's Creek Falls and the scenic crossing of the West Fork just south of Hwy. 28.

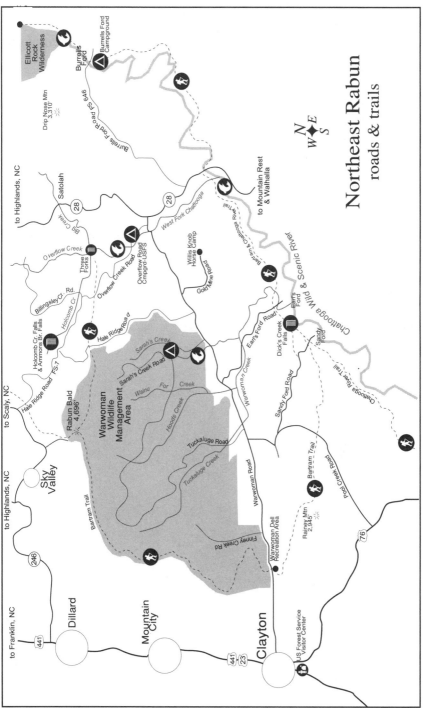

Northeast Rabun
roads & trails

Section Three - National Forest Destinations

Section 4 Four

More **Recreational Destinations**

- Rabun's Great Lakes 100
- Paddling the Tallulah River 105
- Trout Fishing in Rabun 108
- Campgrounds 111
- Foxfire Museum 114
- Tallulah Falls Railroad Museum 115
- Hambidge Center 116
- Barker's Creek Mill 117
- Estatoah and Mud Creek Falls 118
- Ellicott Rock Wilderness 119
- Sightseeing by Auto 120

Rabun's Great Lakes

Five great lakes provide both beauty and recreation

- Lake Burton – elevation 1,867'
- Seed Lake – elevation 1,753'
- Lake Rabun – elevation 1,690'
- Tallulah Lake – elevation 1,500'
- Tugalo Lake – elevation 892'

The northern arm of Lake Burton as viewed from Highway 76.

Rabun County is home to an incomparable string of beautiful mountain lakes. Created by the damming of the Tallulah River in the early 1900s, Rabun's lakes stretch across the southwestern quarter of the county like a string of sparkling manmade jewels. Though created by the Georgia Railway and Power Company with hydroelectric power in mind, the lakes are now known primarily for their upscale homes and outstanding recreational opportunities.

Each of these lakes - Burton, Seed, Rabun, Tallulah and Tugalo are delightfully different in size and personality. They range from the big open water of Lake Burton to the intimate recesses of Tallulah Lake, from the upscale homes lining the shores of Lakes Burton and Rabun to the splendid wilderness of Tugalo Lake. Powerboating, sailing, fishing, skiing, canoeing and swimming are just a few of the leisure time activities that can be enjoyed on Rabun's great lakes.

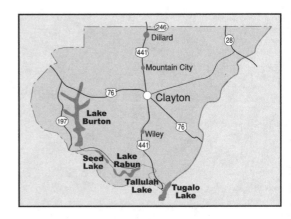

Lake Burton
Surface area: 2,275 acres
Shoreline: 62 miles
Dam: 128' high, 1,100' long
Completion date: 1919

Lake Burton has long been popular with boaters and fishermen. The broadest of the five lakes, Burton features a number of extended arms and secluded coves, offering visitors a wide range of boating experiences. The lake is named for the old settlement of Burton which was submerged upon the lake's impoundment in 1919.

While the overall setting is quite beautiful, the shoreline is heavily developed with private homes and the surrounding mountainsides have lost some of their charm as more and more homes are built. The lake experiences heavy boat use during the summer season as fishermen and pleasure boaters flock to its sparkling cool waters.

Seed Lake
Surface area: 240 acres
Shoreline: 13 miles
Dam: 75' high, 490' long
Completion date: 1926

Seed Lake's narrow shoreline closely follows the Tallulah River's original course through the valley. Seed Lake, also known as Nacoochee Lake, is about 4.5 miles long and is quite popular with area fishermen. Seed's narrow footprint makes it a nice destination for canoeing or paddling, as those areas of the lake exposed to unobstructed wind are minimal.

The lake broadens somewhat as it nears the Nacoochee dam, but it still retains an intimate feel quite different from Burton. Though there are many attractive homes on Seed Lake, the comparitively small size of the lake helps preserve a bit of the wilderness aura here.

Lake Rabun
Surface area: 834 acres
Shoreline: 25 miles
Dam: 108' high, 660' long
Completion date: 1925

There are many who frequent Rabun's lakes that feel Lake Rabun is *the* most beautiful of Georgia's mountain lakes. For over 80 years tourists and seasonal residents have flocked to Lake Rabun, perhaps the most popular of the lakes in the "early days" due to its close proximity to Lakemont, a stop along the old Tallulah Falls Railroad.

Today's Lake Rabun features the same fantastic vistas and is still a great choice both for fishermen and pleasure boaters. Like Burton, Rabun's shoreline is rapidly developing beyond the point most residents would like, but it still retains much of its original mountain charm.

Tallulah Lake
Surface area: 63 acres
Shoreline: 3.6 miles
Dam: 126' high, 426' long
Completion date: 1913

Tallulah Lake was the first of Rabun's lakes along the river. Construction of the Tallulah Falls dam was at the center of a huge conservation battle in the early 1900s between those who wanted hydroelectric power and those parties interested in preserving Tallulah Gorge in its natural state.

Today Tallulah Lake is an important recreational component of Tallulah Gorge State Park. This deep, narrow lake attracts large numbers of bank fishermen, paddlers and swimmers to its scenic sandy beach. The lake is largely undeveloped, though a few pretty homes are situated along the largely wooded banks. Boating is limited to canoes or kayaks.

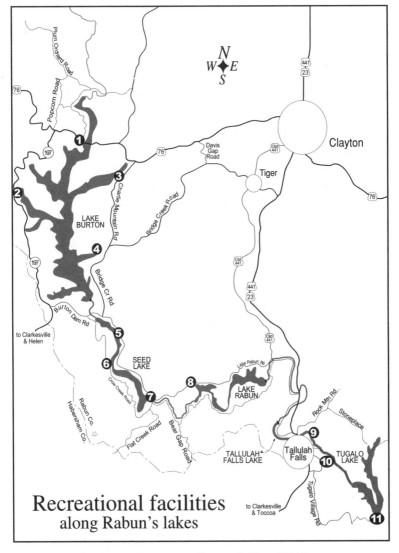

Recreational facilities
along Rabun's lakes

Lakes Recreational Facilities

- **•1 Jones Bridge Park -** sheltered picnic facility overlooking lake
- **•2 Moccasin Creek State Park -** camping, fishing, boating
- **•3 Timpson Cove Beach -** beach, picnic area
- **•4 Murray Cove Boat Launch Area -** paved ramp
- **•5 Lake Seed Boat Launch Area -** gravel ramp
- **•6 Lake Seed Campground -** beach, wilderness camping
- **•7 Nacoochee Park -** picnic area
- **•8 Rabun Beach Recreation Area -** camping, boat ramps, swimming
- **•9 Tallulah Falls State Park -** camping, hiking, swimming, scenery
- **•10 Tallulah Point -** sheltered picnic area
- **•11 Tugalo Park -** camping, boat ramp

Lake Tugalo
Surface area: 597 acres
Shoreline: 18 miles
Dam: 155' high, 940' long
Completion date: 1923

Unlike the other lakes in the Tallulah River chain, Lake Tugalo is a true wilderness lake with virtually no development present other than several boat ramps. Tugalo is formed at the junction of the Tallulah and Chattooga Rivers in the remote and rugged southeastern corner of the county.

Recreation is primarily limited to paddlers and fishermen, and there is a strict limit on the size of boat motors which may be operated here. As strange as it may sound, canoes, kayaks and rafts are frequent visitors to Tugalo. This is because whitewater paddlers who run the Chattooga's legendary Section IV must paddle several miles across Lake Tugalo to access the South Carolina take-out point. The lake is sarcastically referred to as the "world's largest molasses impoundment" by whitewater buffs who had just a short time before had experienced some of the South's best whitewater.

Paddling the Tallulah River

Two separate runs suitable for beginners

- **Upper Tallulah features about 4 miles of easy paddling**
- **Lower Tallulah features 5.5 miles of easy to moderate water**

Low shoals and beautiful scenery on the upper Tallulah River.

Whitewater paddlers from across the country flock to Rabun County to experience the whitewater thrills of the Chattooga Wild and Scenic River (see pages 58-60). But is there anywhere else to paddle in Rabun? Most of the county's streams are small and unnavigable. Besides the Chattooga, the only other river of conseqeunce is the Tallulah; Two distinct sections, separated by three lakes, combine to offer a total of about 10 miles of generally easy to moderate paddling.

Upper Tallulah River

The upper Tallulah offers a 4.3 mile stretch that is generally rated as easy. This spirited run begins along FS 70 near the Tallulah River Campground (be sure not to stray onto private property) and continues down to the bridge at Plum Orchard Road. There are a number of lively shoals scattered

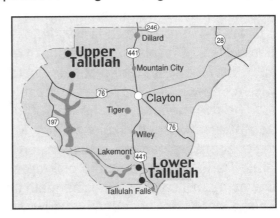

throughout this generally calm but always scenic section. Paddlers who venture downstream of the Plum Orchard bridge will encounter the backwaters of Lake Burton around mile 5 and eventually reach the U.S. 76 bridge at mile 7. Lake paddling always seems to require more energy after you've spent time on the river, but Lake Burton is still worth the effort. At one time paddlers could take out at certain points along Vickers Road, but much of this property is now privately owned.

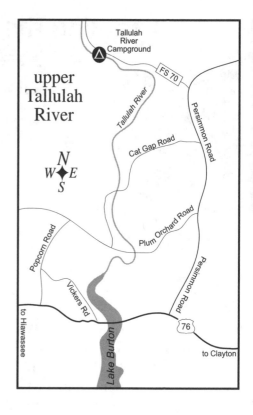

The best advice is to utilize one of the public ramps on the lake such as at Moccasin Creek State Park.

Lower Tallulah River:

This 5.5 mile stretch offers a wide variety of water, and is rated as easy to moderate, though one tricky section rates as a Class 3-4. From the Old Hwy. 441 bridge in Lakemont to the backwaters of Tallulah Lake is about 4 miles. The float is mostly calm with the first sizable shoals occurring at about mile 2.5, where several Class 2 rapids spice things up.

The river negotiates a broad 180-degree bend in the river and passes beneath Highway 441 twice. Just downstream the river passes beneath a suspension bridge in Tallulah Gorge State Park. Things begin to pick up and about one-half mile downstream the river passes beneath the Terrora Circle bridge. This is significant because just downstream the river crashes over a series of respectable ledges. The first one encountered is quite powerful and can easily flip a boat. About 50 yards of whitewater action is all that remains between you and Tallulah Lake, a 63-acre reservoir.

Paddlers may exit the lake at several points along Terrora Circle, but don't be in too big of a hurry. Tallulah Lake is quite pretty and features several scenic creeks which cascade into its calm waters. You may even want to paddle down to the beach and picnic area before heading for home.

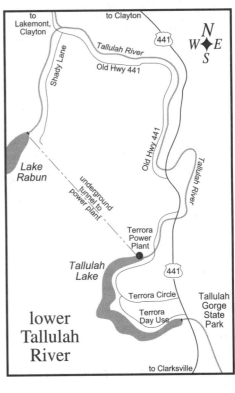

Tallulah Gorge State Park Whitewater Releases

Several weekends each year, Tallulah Gorge is turned into a whitewater mecca as the floodgates atop the dam are opened and the river returns to its 19th century glory.

This is experts-only whitewater and the 2+ mile run includes several respectable waterfalls - Oceana, Bridal Veil and Sweet Sixteen.

To view boaters running the rapids of Tallulah Gorge, be sure to visit the first few weekends of April and November. Releases are held on Saturday and Sunday. While not just anyone can run the rapids of Tallulah Gorge, anyone can make the short hike out to a rim overlook and enjoy the view. For more information, call the park or visit their website (see pages 10-17).

Trout Fishing

Rabun streams are among Georgia's best for trout fishing

- **Georgia residents 16–65 must have a state fishing license and trout stamp**
- **Georgia residents over 65 may receive a free honorary license**
- **Seasonal streams open from the last Saturday in March through the end of October**

Trout fishing on rugged Overflow Creek.

One of Rabun's most popular outdoor activities is fishing. Literally thousands of anglers enjoy our beautiful lakes, rivers and streams each year. Yet perhaps the most dedicated members of this clan are trout fishermen. These hardy souls brave the elements on Rabun's excellent assortment of trout waters. Whether it is the grace and skill of the fly fisherman or the simplicity of fishing from the riverbank, there's a stream in Rabun to suit your tastes.

Year-round streams

Chattooga River: No special regulations. The upper Chattooga from Russell bridge north to Burrells Ford is a very popular section. The farther you walk from a bridge the more likely you are to escape the crowds. The Chattooga is normally quite wide, unlike nearly every other trout stream in the county. Brook, rainbow and brown trout are regularly stocked along this section.

West Fork Chattooga River: No special regulations. The West Fork is a favorite of Rabun trout anglers. Accessible from the Chattooga north to upstream of the Overflow Road campground, the West Fork is fairly broad and somewhat easy to fish. Normally stocked weekly through the summer.

Tallulah River: No special regulations. The crowds on the upper Tallulah will rival or surpass any stream in the county. The river is heavily stocked weekly through the summer. Three USFS campgrounds are located on FS 70 (Tallulah River Road), the road which closely parallels the river upstream.

Overflow Creek: No special regulations. A good deal of fast water in a rugged wilderness environment. From Warwoman Road, follow FS 86 (Overflow Road) for six miles. Turn right onto FS 86B and drive 3 miles to the creek.

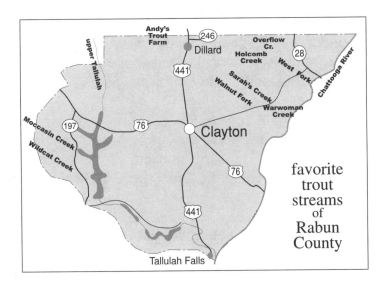

Seasonal streams

Holcomb Creek: No special regulations. A significant West Fork tributary stream, a portion of Holcomb Creek flows alongside Hale Ridge Road above the FS 7 / FS 86 intersection. Normally stocked 6-8 times during the summer.

Sarah's Creek: No special regulations. Popular stream in the Warwoman WMA. Good access along Sarah's Creek Road. From Clayton, take Wawoman Road east for 8 miles. Turn left onto Sarah's Creek Road and drive up to the ford. A USFS campground is located here as well.

Seasonal streams - continued

Walnut Fork and Hood Creek: Artificial lures only. Tight, intimate small stream setting. Follow directions to Sarah's Creek ford. Cross, then turn left onto FS 155. Drive 1.5 miles to Walnut Fork. Walnut Fork merges with Hood Creek about one mile downstream.

Warwoman Creek: No special regulations. Take Warwoman Road east for 5 miles and turn right onto Earl's Ford Road. Proceed one mile to the creek.

Moccasin Creek: Special regulations: Wildcat Creek within the park is reserved for senior citizens and children. That portion on USFS land upstream of the park is open to the public.

Wildcat Creek: No special regulations. Popular stream in the Lake Burton WMA. Regularly stocked. Good access along West Wildcat Creek Road (FS 26). Two USFS campgrounds in the area.

Andy's Trout Farm: Just in case you get skunked, don't let your pride get the best of you. Andy's Trout Farm is just up the road near Dillard. Andy's has several ponds absolutely loaded with trout, and you pay for what you catch. If you're taking trout home for dinner the wife will never know. Pole rentals are available. Normally open April 1 through Thanksgiving. Call (706) 746-2550. From Hwy. 441 in Dillard, take Betty's Creek Road west for 5 miles.

If you really want to find out about Rabun trout, you may want to obtain a copy of Tony Wheeler's humorous book, *"Trout Fishing for Tourists in Georgia's Rabun County."* Enquire locally for a copy.

Campgrounds

Rabun County offers many scenic options for campers

- Seasonal and year-round campgrounds
- Forest Service campgrounds
- Georgia Power campgrounds
- State Park campgrounds

Note: Be aware that most campgrounds experience heavy use during warm weather weekends and throughout the summer season.

There's just nothing quite like camping to get you into the spirit of the great outdoors, and Rabun County offers a wide variety of campgrounds ranging from bare-bones primitive to fully developed state park facilities. Whether your preference is pup-tent or travel trailer, we've got you covered.

US Forest Service campgrounds

Rabun Beach Recreation Area: Open late April through October. The largest USFS campground in the Chattahoochee National Forest features 80 campsites. Approximately 20 of these sites include electricity and water hookups. Rabun Beach campground features a bath house with hot showers and flush toilets. Basic site is $12 per night; sites with electricity and water are $20 per night. Take Old Hwy. 441 to Lake Rabun Road. Proceed 5 miles to the campground.

Wildcat Creek I & II: Open year round. Each site features 16 campgrounds along scenic Wildcat Creek. No drinking water. Vault toilets. Wildcat I (lower campground) is $8 per night; Wildcat II is $6 per night. Located along West Wildcat Creek Road off Hwy. 197.

Tallulah River: Open from late March through October. Features 17 campsites along the beautiful upper Tallulah River. Drinking water and vault toilets. Sites are $14 per night. The campground is located on the lower end of Tallulah River Road (FS 70). From Clayton, take Hwy. 76 west for 8 miles. Turn right onto Persimmon Road and proceed 4 miles to Tallulah River Road on the left.

Tate Branch: Open from late March through October. Features 19 campsites along the upper Tallulah River. Drinking water and vault toilets. Sites are $12 per night. Follow directions to Tallulah River campground and proceed an additonal 3 miles up Tallulah River Road.

Sandy Bottoms: Open year-round. Features 12 campsites along the upper Tallulah. Drinking water and vault toilets. Sites are $12 per night. Follow directions to Tate Branch, then proceed about one mile further along Tallulah River Road.

Sarah's Creek: Open year-round. Features 28 sites along Sarah's Creek. No drinking water; vault toilets. Sites are $4 per night. From Clayton, take Warwoman Road east for 7 miles. Turn left onto Sarah's Creek Road and drive 2 miles to the campground.

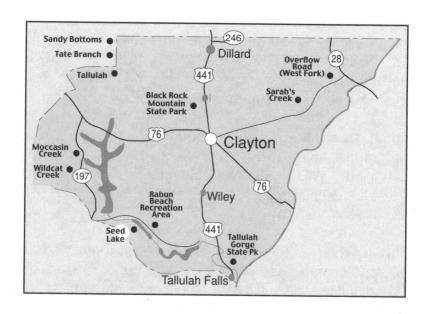

Overflow Road (aka West Fork): Open year-round. Primitive camping area along the West Fork features 5 sites. No drinking water; vault toilet. From Clayton, take Warwoman Road east for 13 miles. Turn left onto Overflow Road (FS 86) and proceed one mile.

State Park campgrounds:
Black Rock Mountain State Park: Georgia's highest park features a 48 tent and trailer sites, a walk-in camping area and several backcountry sites. Located just west of Mountain City off Hwy. 441. Call (706) 746-2141 for rates and availability or visit www.gastateparks.org.

Tallulah Gorge State Park: Dramatic Tallulah Gorge State Park offers 50 tent and trailer sites. Located just east of Hwy. 441 off Jane Hurt Yarn Road. Call (706) 754-7970 for rates and availability or go online at www.gastateparks.org.

Moccasin Creek State Park: Pretty Moccasin Creek State Park features 54 tent and trailer campsites along beautiful Lake Burton. Located on Hwy. 197 about 30 minutes north of Clarkesville. Call (706) 947-3194 for rates or go to the state parks website at www.gastateparks.org.

Georgia Power campground
Lake Seed Campground: Call for seasons of operation. Located on the back side of Seed Lake, this camping area features restrooms and a beach. Contact the Georgia Power Land Management Office for more information (706) 782-4014. Camping reservations: (706) 754-7979 or (888) GPCLAKE.

Private campgrounds: There are several privately owned campgrounds in Rabun County. Call the Rabun County Chamber of Commerce for information (706) 782-4812.

Foxfire Farm & Museum

Preserving Appalachian history and culture

Foxfire Museum
P.O. Box 541
Mountain City, GA 30562
(706) 746–5828

- **Historic structures**
- **Visitor center on Hwy. 441**
- **Gift shop & tours**
- **Nature trail**
- **Fee required**

A restored Appalachian church at the Foxfire Center.

The world-renowned Foxfire program originated in Rabun County in 1966 with *Foxfire Magazine*, a creative attempt to motivate high school English students towards greater learning. Today, 40 years and over 8.5 million books later, Foxfire continues as a leader in the learner-centered, community-based educational approach.

The Foxfire farm features an impressive collection of over 20 authentic log structures and a fascinating display of Appalachian tools and equipment in a functional farm setting. After your tour be sure to visit the gift shop where a collection of pottery, soaps and books (including the *Foxfire* collection) is offered.

Directions: From the highway in Mountain City, take Black Rock Mtn. Pkwy. for 1 mile. Turn left onto Down Home Lane. Proceed to the stop, then bear left onto Cross Street. Drive 0.5 mile and turn right onto Foxfire Lane.

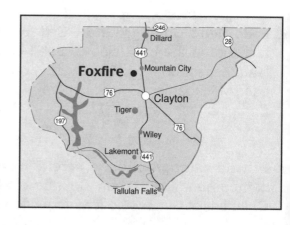

Tallulah Falls Railroad Museum
Commemorating the historic "Total Failure" Railroad

- **Normal hours: Friday, Saturday & Sunday Spring through Fall**
- **(706) 746-7467 (Rabun Gap-Nachoochee School number)**
- **Nominal admission fee**

Everything here was built by Dess Oliver and his RGNS students.

The magnificent Tallulah Falls Railroad was one of the most unique shortline railroads ever constructed. The Old TF ran 58 scenic miles over 42 wonderful wooden trestles from Cornelia, Georgia to Franklin, North Carolina. Constructed primarily between 1898 and 1905, the railroad was abandoned in 1961 because of ongoing financial difficulties.

During its operation, the TF carried thousands of passengers and "opened up" the isolated mountain area to development. The line was so unique that several movies including Disney's "The Great Locomotive Chase" were filmed here. Dess Oliver, Industrial Arts instructor at Rabun Gap-Nacoochee School, along with his students, lovingly built this museum, including the full size two-foot gauge locomotive and cars. The museum is filled with scores of authentic TFRR relics and photos.

Directions: The museum is located 5 minutes north of Clayton on Hwy. 441 (between Rabun Gap and Dillard), directly across from historic Rabun Gap-Nacoochee School.

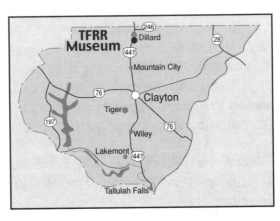

Hambidge Center

Dedicated to the preservation of mountain arts

The Hambidge Center
P.O. Box 339
Rabun Gap, GA 30568
(706) 746-5718
www.hambidge.org

- Artist retreat
- Arts center
- Gift shop
- Walking trails

The Hambidge Center's arched springhouse.

This renowned 600-acre preserve is dedicated to the preservation of mountain arts and crafts. Founded by Mary Hambidge, an early environmentalist and mountain culture preservationist, the Hambidge Center features a gallery, workshop, dining hall and several cabins. Mary Hambidge had a history of encouraging local artists and crafters, particularly in the disciplines of dyeing and weaving. Hambidge earned great recognition by developing a range of vegetable dyes.

A wide variety of programs are offered during the spring, summer and fall seasons. Workshops, seminars and other programs are regularly featured. Each year the Hambidge Center awards several dozen resident fellowships to artists from across the country and around the world who come to this beautiful setting to spur their creative processes.

Check with the center for hours of operation. Visitors are asked to register in the main office, but are normally welcome to roam about on the property's nature trails.

Directions: From Hwy. 441 in Dillard, turn west onto Betty's Creek Road and proceed 4 miles to the Hambidge Center on the right.

Barker's Creek Mill

These early structures were once the centers of their communities

Owned and operated by the Hambidge Center

- **Historic grist mill**
- **Picnic table**
- **Normally open and operational on warm weather weekends**

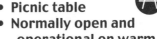

The beautiful setting at Barker's Creek Mill.

ocated on the expansive grounds of the Hambidge Center, this unique structure is a rare throwback to the days when these water powered marvels were the commercial centers of isolated, rural mountain communities.

Barker's Creek Mill was constructed in 1944 for Hambidge Center founder Mary Hambidge. Several other mills were built on or near Betty's Creek over the past 170 years, but Barker's Creek Mill is the only one that has survived. The mill is normally open to the public on warm weather weekends, and usually grinds corn meal the first weekend of each month. This peaceful, rustic setting is a great spot to picnic along the banks of splashing Barker's Creek. Check at the Hambidge Center office for exact times of operation.

Directions: Follow the directions to the Hambidge Center. To reach the mill, continue west on Betty's Crek Road for an additional mile. Look for the mill sign and pull-off on the left.

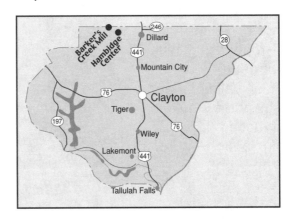

Estatoah & Mud Creek Falls

Two scenic falls that can be enjoyed from your vehicle

Estatoah Falls is a large, open cascade easily visible from Highway 246 just east of Dillard. This enormous waterfall is privately owned, and waterfall enthusiasts must settle for admiring Estatoah's beauty from afar. The cascade occurs on Mud Creek as it tumbles several hundred feet from the heavily wooded mountain slopes below Sky Valley. The waterfall is pretty at any time of the year, but after a heavy rain Estatoah literally explodes from the the sheer grey cliffs.

Directions: From Dillard, follow GA 246 east toward Sky Valley. After about one mile, look ahead, just to the right and you will see the fall's lower cascades.

Another prominent waterfall in the Sky Valley area is formed on the same creek as Estatoah Falls. While the name **Mud Creek Falls** doesn't do much for the imagination, this is a real sleeper among Rabun cascades. Mud Creek Falls tumbles over a jagged 60-foot ledge and features a wild "roostertail" of water that leaps outward from the cliff face at high water levels.

Directions: From Dillard, take GA 246 for 4.3 miles. Turn right at the Sinclair gas station. Proceed 0.9 mile and turn right into Sky Valley. Bear left at the stop and proceed 0.55 mile to Tahoe Road on the right. Drive 0.75 mile to the base of the falls.

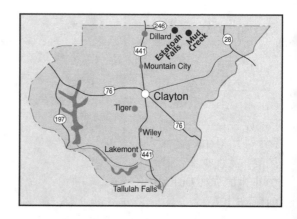

Ellicott Rock Wilderness
Beautiful wilderness area along the upper Chattooga River

- Miles of hiking trails
- Wilderness camping
- Fishing on the Chattooga River
- Strict regulations regarding usage

A relatively small portion of the beautiful Ellicott Rock Wilderness lies in Rabun County, and if wilderness is what you come to the mountains for, ERW is the place for you. This 9,000+ acre reserve was established in the 1970s and encompasses much of the dynamic area where GA, SC and NC join. This is true wilderness - if you want to explore here, it will have to be on foot.

The incomparable Chattooga River bisects the heart of ERW and several excellent trails traverse the rugged ridges and peaks found here. Unfortunately, none of the established trails are in Rabun County. The good news, however, is that all of these pathways are within easy reach of northeast Rabun.

Check with the U.S. Forest Service office in Clayton for detailed maps and other publications detailing Ellicott Rock Wilderness.

Directions:
Ellicott Rock Wilderness can be accessed from Burrells Ford, the Walhalla Fish Hatchery off Hwy. 107 in SC, or from Bull Pen Road (also off Hwy. 107) in NC. See area map on page 34.

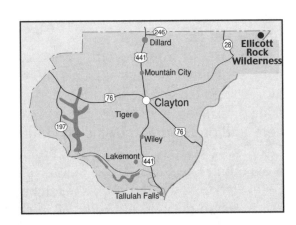

Sightseeing by Auto

There's a lot to see from the comfort of your car

A great deal of Rabun County's world-class scenery is easily visible from the comfort of your automobile. Just pick up a map of the county and take off. You can take a grand tour that includes rivers, lakes and mountains in just a few short hours. Plan your own route or pick one of the ones listed below. If you try one of the ones listed here, be aware that all mileage given is approximate due to variables involved in any auto trip. See county map on page 8.

Lakes Tour: Approximately 40 miles. This drive features lake vistas, scenic mountain overlooks, trails, marinas, parks and a number of interesting shops.

From Clayton, take Old Hwy. 441 south for about 8 miles to historic Lakemont, one of the stops on the old Tallulah Falls Railroad. Turn right onto Lake Rabun Road and follow the winding road around Lake Rabun's northern shoreline, which features numerous shops, inns and upscale homes. After about 4 miles you will come to Rabun Beach Recreation Area, then several miles later you'll see Nacoochee Park just below the Seed Lake dam.

Lake Rabun Road becomes Seed Lake Road and continues northwest along the narrow lake's shoreline. The road crosses the Tallulah River below Burton dam, then proceeds several additional miles up to an intersection with Hwy. 197. Turn right here and proceed approximately 8 miles up the west side of Lake Burton. Though lake views are somewhat limited, there are a number of good access points, primarily Moccasin Creek State Park and the Burton Fish Hatchery.

Continue north to the Hwy. 76 intersection. Turn left and

follow the road out to Popcorn Overlook. Go a few miles more and you'll come to Dick's Creek Gap and a junction with the Appalachian Trail.

Turn around and proceed east on Hwy. 76 past Hwy. 197 and across the upper arm of Lake Burton. From here it's about 10 miles back to Clayton. Be sure to take a county map with you, as there are many side roads that feature interesting stops along this route.

Chattooga River - Warwoman Loop: Approximately 40 miles. Features beautiful valley scenery and the Chattooga River.

Take Hwy. 76 east from Clayton for 9 miles to the Chattooga River bridge. Enter South Carolina and proceed several miles up to Chattooga Ridge Road on the left. Follow this long winding road up to a 4-way stop sign at Whetstone Road. To the left Earl's Ford Road heads west to a parking area just a short walk from the Chattooga River.

Backtrack to the 4-way stop, then head north on Chattooga Ridge Road for several miles up to the intersection with Hwy. 28. Turn left and climb to Callas Gap in the Sumter National Forest, then descend to the Chattooga River in the Long Bottom Ford area. You will pass the Long Bottom Ford boat launch site, then historic Russell farmstead just before crossing the Chattooga River and reentering Georgia.

Continue along Hwy. 28 past Russell bridge for 2 miles and turn left onto Warwoman Road. From here it is approximately 14 miles back to Clayton. Locations of particular interest along the road back include the West Fork Chattooga River (about 0.2 miles from Hwy. 28) and Warwoman Dell, just a few miles east of Clayton.

Persimmon - Patterson Gap Loop: Approximately 30 miles. Features open mountain valleys, forested coves and scenic splashing creeks, and lots of isolation on Patterson Gap Road.

From Clayton, take Hwy. 441 north to Dillard, then turn left onto Betty's Creek Road. Proceed through this beautiful valley for about 3 miles to Patterson Gap Road on the left (You may

Sightseeing by Auto – continued

wish to continue straight ahead on Betty's Creek Road first to take in the sights at the Hambidge Center and Andy's Trout Farm). Follow Patterson Gap Road (FS 32) for 3 miles up to Patterson Gap, then descend approximately 4 miles down into the beautiful Persimmon valley. Note: Patterson Gap Road is a single-lane gravel Forest Service Road, and as such can be quite muddy and bumpy.

Proceed south to Persimmon Road. Take Persimmon Road south for about 5 miles back to the intersection with Hwy. 76. Turn left and proceed 8 miles back to Clayton.

Upper Tallulah - Tate City: Approximately 40 miles. Features the beautiful river gorge of the upper Tallulah River and excellent mountain vistas from the Tate City area.

From Clayton, take Hwy. 76 west for 8 miles. Turn right onto Persimmon Road and drive 4 miles to Tallulah River Road on the left. Tallulah River Road heads north for 9 miles (most of it gravel), terminating about 2 miles north of the North Carolina line deep in the Southern Nantahala Wilderness.

The most dramatic portion of this drive is the 3 mile section of FS 70 directly alongside the plunging river in the dramatic Rock Mountain Gorge. This section of the roadway once held a narrow gauge railroad built to carry timber from logging operations around the Tate City area, and the roadbed was literally blasted into the steep mountainside. Keep your eyes open, as numerous streams cascade into the churning Tallulah from high above.

Beyond the gorge the road traverses the wide, peaceful valley known as Tate City. Home to farms, fields and a growing number of homes, Tate City is a stark contrast to the dramatic scenery of Rock Mountain Gorge. Above Tate City, the valley narrows once again, and the road ends about 2 miles beyond the North Carolina line at a series of hiking trailheads. Turn around here and retrace your route back to Clayton.

Section Five

Additional Information

Emergency Numbers

Police • Fire • Ambulance • Rescue   **911**
   (all locations in Rabun County)

Rabun County Hospital
   196 Ridgecrest Circle, Clayton   **782–4233**

Georgia State Patrol – Toccoa   **1–706–282–4531**

Department of Natural Resources **1–800–241–4113**

Additional Information

(all area codes 706 unless otherwise stated)

Campgrounds & RV Parks (commercial)

Andy's Trout Farm

    Betty's Creek Road, Dillard   746-2550

Dillard RV Park

    Franklin Street, Dillard   746-2713

Camp Rainey Mountain (Boy Scouts)

    Rainey Mountain Road, Clayton   782-3733

Mr. Bud's

    Hwy. 197 North, Batesville   947-3420

Mountain City RV Park

    618 File Street, Mountain City   490-0161

River Vista RV Resort

    960 Hwy. 246, Dillard   746-2722

Chattooga River Rafting

Nantahala Outdoor Center   (704) 488-6900

    Chattooga Ridge Rd., Mtn. Rest, SC   (800) 232-7238

Southeastern Expeditions   (404) 329-0433

    Hwy. 76 East, Clayton   (800) 868-7238

Wildwater, Ltd.   (864) 647-9587

    Long Creek, SC   (800) 451-9972

Chattooga Whitewater Shop

    Hwy. 76, Long Creek, SC   (864) 647-9083

Golf – Public Courses

Kingwood Resort

    Hwy. 76 East   212-4100

Rabun County Golf Club

    Hwy. 441 South   782-5500

Sky Valley Golf Course   746-5303

Horseback Riding

Dillard House Stables   746-5348

Circle R Trails   (864) 638-0115

Marinas and Boat Dealers

Anchorage Boat Dock - Lake Burton	782-5193
Hwy. 76 West	
Anchorage Marine	782-3013
Hall's Boat House - Lake Rabun	
Lake Rabun Road, Lakemont	782-2628
Lakemont Marine - Lake Rabun	
1897 Lake Rabun Rd., Lakemont	782-4981
Lake Rabun Marina	
5628 Lake Rabun Rd., Lakemont	782-4936
Mark's Marine - Lake Burton	
Hwy. 76 West	782-5565

Rabun County Chamber of Commerce

and Welcome Center, 232 Hwy. 441 N	782-5113

Skiing and Snow Tubing

Scaly Mountain Tubing Area	(704) 526-3737
Hwy. 106, Scaly, N.C.	(800) 929-7669
Sky Valley Resort	746-5302
	(800) 437-2416

Trout Fishing

Andy's Trout Farm	
Betty's Creek Road, Dillard	746-2550

U.S. Forest Service

Hwy. 441 South, Clayton	782-3320

Seasonal Special Events

Check with the Rabun County Chamber of Commerce for exact dates. (706) 782-4812 or go to www.gamountains.com and click "calendar".

April
- Tallulah Gorge State Park Whitewater Release
  1st two weekends
- Celebrate Clayton - Arts and Crafts festival

May
- Foxfire Community Celebration
  Saturday before Mother's Day
  746-5828

June
- Pottery shows - The Hambidge Center
  746-5989
- Lake Burton Fun Run
  782-4812

July
- 4th of July Fireworks - Dillard
- 4th of July Fireworks - Lake Rabun and Lake Burton

August
- Dillard Bluegrass & Barbeque Festival
  Dillard City Hall
- "His Last Days" Outdoor Drama
  Tallulah Gallery - Tallulah Falls Scenic Loop

September
- Rhapsody in Rabun Charity Event
  live music, dancing, silent auction, gourmet food
  782-2034

October

- Harvest Sale - Dillard
  weekends through October
- Homemaker's Sale - Dillard Farmer's Market
  arts, crafts and harvest goods
- Halloween Heyday - Clayton
  Saturday closest to Halloween. Kids parade and party

November

- Veteran's Day Celebration - Clayton
  782-7970
- Member's Art Showcase - Talluah Falls
  Heritage Center for the Arts
  runs through December 754-5989

December

- Chamber of Commerce Christmas Parade
  Main Street in Clayton - call for date and time
- Christmas Tour of Homes
  Sponsored by the Rabun County Board of Realtors
  782-7751

"Trust in the Lord with all your heart,
And lean not on your own understanding;
In all your ways acknowledge Him,
And He shall direct your paths."
Proverbs 3:5-6